Table of Contents

Chapter 1: Industry Overview

For Those Interested in the Insurance Industry	2
Insurance: Financial Protection From Risks	3
By the Numbers	3
How Insurers Make Money	5
The Economics of Insurance	6
How Insurance Is Sold	7
Important Functions of Insurance Organizations	9
Insurance Entities	11

Chapter 2: Property/Casualty

Property/Casualty Market at a Glance	16
Property/Casualty Coverage Types and Lines of Business	18
Commercial Lines of Business	20

Chapter 3: Life

Life Market at a Glance	26
Life Insurers Chasing Wider Range of Opportunities	28
Important Lines of Life Business and Products	30
Annuity Products	31
Accident & Health Products	33

Chapter 4: Health

Health Market at a Glance	37
Developing Issues for Health Insurers	37
Major Types of Health Plans	39
Products and Terms	40
Common Health Insurance Terms	41

Chapter Risk Transfer

Overview of Reinsurance	44
Developing Issues in Reinsurance	45
Alternative Risk Transfer and Risk Financing	46
Insurance-Linked Securities and Structured Transactions	47

Chapter 6: Fiscal Fitness & AM Best

Insurance Stands the Traditional Business Cycle on Its Head	54
The Risk of Financial Impairment	55
Overview: Best's Credit Rating Evaluation	56
AM Best's Insurance Information Products and Services	58

Spotlights

On High Alert: Rising Risks of PFAS Claims and Litigation Capture New Attention	13
Insurers Turn to Apprenticeships	14
Strength Through Specialization	22
Independent Streak	24
Cryptocurrency: Insurance Industry Tests the Waters With New Initiatives	34
A Healthy Dose of Reality	42
Winds of Change: Derechos, Snowstorms and Other Catastrophes Are Becoming a Growing Problem for Insurers	49
Laboratory of the Minds	52
The Greening of Insurance Asset Management	62

BEST'S GUIDE TO UNDERSTANDING THE INSURANCE INDUSTRY
2021 Edition

Published by AM Best

AM BEST COMPANY, INC.
Oldwick, NJ
CHAIRMAN, PRESIDENT & CEO Arthur Snyder III
SENIOR VICE PRESIDENTS Alessandra L. Czarnecki, Thomas J. Plummer
GROUP VICE PRESIDENT Lee McDonald

AM BEST RATING SERVICES, INC.
Oldwick, NJ
PRESIDENT & CEO Matthew C. Mosher
EXECUTIVE VICE PRESIDENT & COO James Gillard
EXECUTIVE VICE PRESIDENT & CSO Andrea Keenan
SENIOR MANAGING DIRECTORS Edward H. Easop, Stefan W. Holzberger, James F. Snee

ART & PRODUCTION
SENIOR MANAGER Susan L. Browne
DESIGN/GRAPHICS Angel M. Negrón

Tell Us What You Think
Is this publication helpful to you?
Did you find the information you were looking for?
What other information do you wish we had included?
Send your thoughts to *news@ambest.com*.

Copyright © 2021 AM Best Company, Inc. and/or its affiliates. ALL RIGHTS RESERVED. No portion of this content may be reproduced, distributed, or stored in a database or retrieval system, or transmitted in any form or by any means without the prior written permission of AM Best. While the content was obtained from sources believed to be reliable, its accuracy is not guaranteed. For additional details, refer to our *Terms of Use* available at AM Best website: *www.ambest.com/terms*.

ISSN 2375-7280

Visit *http://guides.ambest.com* to order additional copies.

For Those Interested in the Insurance Industry

AM Best publishes *Understanding the Insurance Industry* to provide a clear picture of how the insurance industry operates, generates revenue and provides opportunities for people of varied talents and interests.

It's designed to provide readers with a high-level overview of the insurance industry, particularly how it operates in the United States. It's also designed to be a gentle and broad introduction to the insurance industry for students, new employees, prospects and those who would like to learn more about one of the most interesting and important financial services industries.

We've designed this book in six sections: the property/casualty sector (also known as nonlife insurance), life, health, reinsurance and alternative risk transfer, and the function of AM Best in the industry.

Articles were prepared by members of AM Best's editorial team. Some content is extracted from Special Reports produced by AM Best, from articles in *Best's Review* magazine and from reporting specifically for this edition.

Additional copies of this book are available by ordering online. If you have suggestions for future topics or areas of focus, please send your comments to *news@ambest.com*.

Even more information, including monthly analytic broadcasts, topical webinars and other multiplatform resources are available at *www.ambest.com*.

CHAPTER 1: INDUSTRY OVERVIEW

Insurance: Financial Protection From Risks

Insurance protects against the financial risks that are present at all stages of people's lives and businesses. Insurers protect against loss — of a car, a house, even a life—and pay the policyholder or designee a benefit in the event of that loss. Those who suffer the loss present a claim and request payment under the insurance coverage terms, which are outlined in a policy. Insurers typically cannot replace the item lost but can provide financial compensation to address the economic hardship caused by a loss.

All aspects of life include exposure to risk. Individuals and businesses are presented with a choice: Accept the consequences of a possible loss, or seek insurance coverage in the event of a loss, reducing the exposure to risk. Those who don't procure insurance coverage are responsible for the full loss. Those who obtain coverage succeed in "transferring the risk" to another organization, typically an insurance company.

Purchasing insurance is the most common risk transfer mechanism for the majority of people and organizations. The money paid from the insured is known as the premium. In return, the insurer agrees to pay a designated benefit in the event of the agreed-upon loss.

By the Numbers

Insurance takes advantage of concepts known as risk pooling and the law of large numbers. Many policyholders pay a relatively small amount in premiums to protect themselves against a possible larger loss. When a sufficient number of insureds make that same choice, the funds available to pay claims increase and the chances of any single person or group exhausting the available funds grow smaller.

In risk pooling, insurers can accept a diverse and large number of risks, so long as many people participate in the insurance process, and the insured risks are individually unpredictable and infrequent. Although an insurer may accept risks from a large number of people, only a small portion of those are likely to suffer an insured financial loss during the period of insurance coverage. Risk pooling allows insurers to pay claims to the few from the funds of the many.

What insurers sell is protection against economic loss. These losses are outlined in contracts or documents known as insurance policies. Insurers that cover life and health usually do not cover property or liability, which is the domain of property/casualty insurers.

Life and health insurers cover three general areas:

- Protection against premature death.
- Protection against poor health or unexpected medical costs.
- Protection against outliving one's financial resources.

CHAPTER 1: INDUSTRY OVERVIEW

Nonlife insurers, known as the property/casualty sector in the United States and Canada, in general offer two basic forms of coverage:

- Property insurance provides protection against most risks to tangible property occurring as the result of collision, fire, flood, earthquake, theft or other perils.
- Casualty, or liability, insurance is broader than property and is often coverage of an individual or organization for negligent acts or omissions.

A well-known form of casualty insurance, auto liability coverage, protects drivers in the event they are found to be at fault in an accident.

A driver found to be at fault may be responsible for medical expenses, repairs and restitution to other people involved in the incident.

Insurance Density – Annual Per Capita Insurance Premiums (2020)

Source: Swiss Re *sigma* and Axco

CHAPTER 1: INDUSTRY OVERVIEW

How Insurers Make Money

Insurance companies primarily make money in two ways: from investments and by generating an underwriting profit—that is, collecting premium that exceeds insured losses and related expenses.

It all begins with underwriting. Insurers, whether life or nonlife, must assess the risk and gauge the likelihood of claims and the value of those claims.

Insurance companies invest assets that are set aside to pay claims brought by policyholders. The interval between the time the insurer receives the premium and the time a claim against that policy is made is known as the "float."

If an insurer has predominantly short-term obligations, asset portfolios should be relatively liquid in nature (i.e., publicly traded bonds, commercial paper and cash).

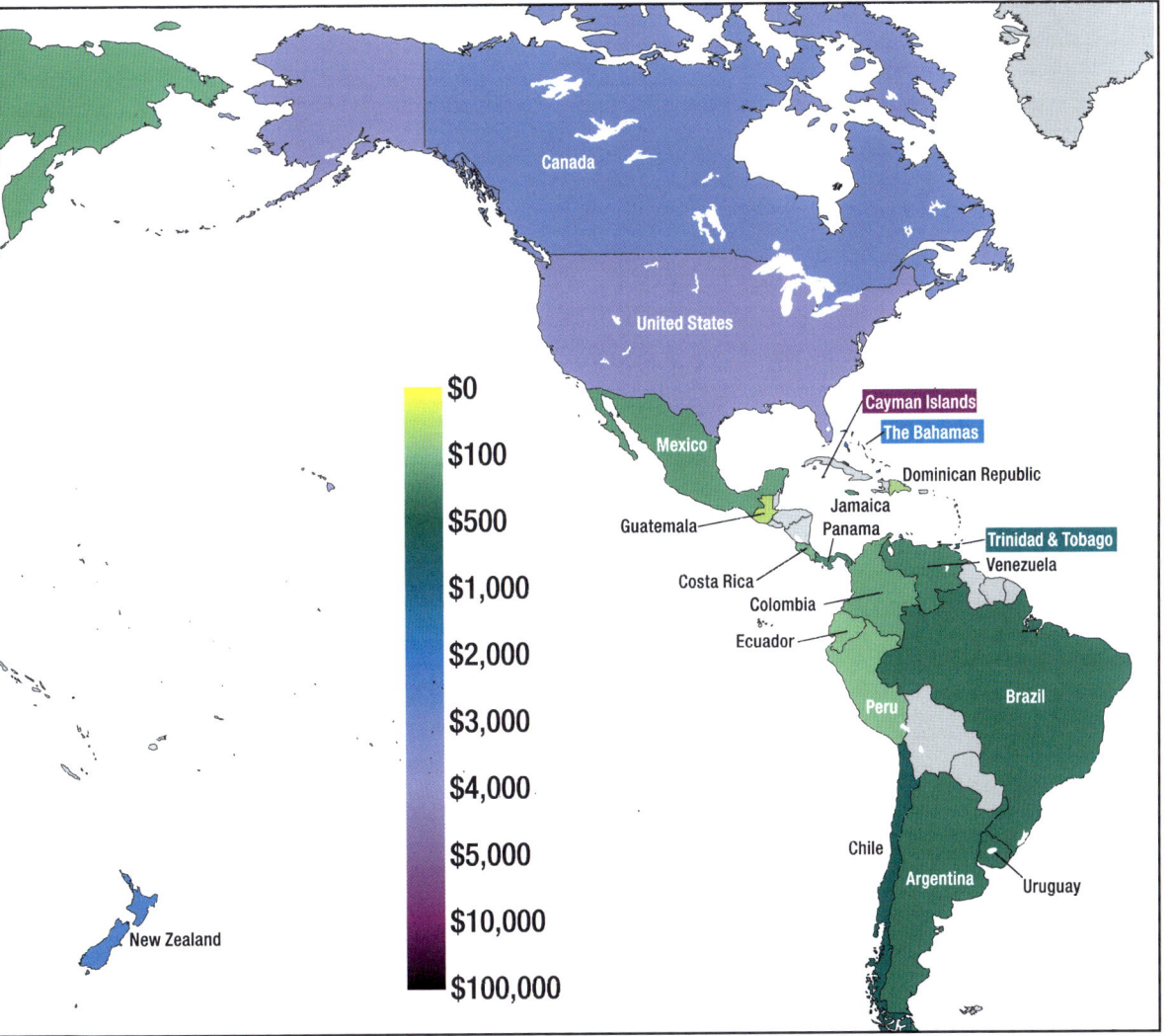

www.ambest.com

CHAPTER 1: INDUSTRY OVERVIEW

If the needs are long term, a portfolio containing fixed-income securities, such as bonds and mortgage loans, may also include preferred and common stocks, real estate and a variety of alternative asset classes.

Life insurers also establish separate accounts for nonguaranteed insurance products, such as variable life insurance or annuities, which provide for investment decisions by policyholders.

Property/casualty insurers traditionally have been more conservative with the asset side of their balance sheets, primarily due to the high levels of risk on the liability side. For example, catastrophe losses can wipe out years of accumulated premiums in some lines.

In the end, the insurer builds up a diversified portfolio of financial assets that will eventually be used to pay off any future claims brought by policyholders.

The global recession of the previous decade hurt nearly all aspects of the insurance industry, as many companies experienced declining revenues and investment losses. Companies that were trading riskier instruments such as credit default swaps suffered most severely.

Few winners emerged. However, the mutual insurance sector managed to remain somewhat unscathed by the downturn. Meanwhile, a chronic low interest rate environment limited the ability of life and other insurers to benefit from fixed investments such as bonds. That may be changing, depending on economic conditions that could spur higher inflation.

The Economics of Insurance

More than 2,603 single property/casualty companies and 752 single life/health insurance companies are included in AM Best's files for the United States and Canada. AM Best's global database includes information on more than 10,812 insurance companies worldwide. Insurers pay claims in property, liability, life, health, annuity, reinsurance and other forms of coverage. In the United States alone, the broader insurance industry provides employment to 2.8 million people.

US Insurance Industry Jobs by Sector – 2021

Life and health insurance carriers	957,900
Insurance agencies and brokerages	869,800
Direct property and casualty insurers	557,400
Third-party administration of insurance funds	198,100
Title insurance and other direct insurance carriers	105,900
Claims adjusting	57,200
Reinsurance carriers	25,600

Source: U.S. Department of Labor, Bureau of Labor Statistics

Insurance organizations play a vital role in the U.S. and other economies. They protect individuals and businesses from financial loss. Money they receive as premiums is invested in the economy. Protection from financial loss provides a sense of security to individuals and businesses, which are freer to pursue business and personal opportunities with less worry about financial devastation. Businesses can

afford to purchase real estate and equipment, to hire more employees and fund travel and expansion.

Premiums collected from insureds, often known as policyholders, are invested by insurance organizations until they are paid out. Investor Warren Buffett has famously championed the value of "float"—funds held by insurance companies until they must be paid—as an important source of investment capital. However, insurers must be cautious and risk-averse with the majority of their investments, both to satisfy regulators' demands and to be able at any moment to pay claims.

Insurance companies are large holders of bonds, particularly those issued by corporations and similar sources. They invest small portions of their available funds in stocks. Life insurers have traditionally played larger roles in real estate investments, although a portion of those investments has shifted from direct ownership of commercial properties to more liquid investments in real estate investment trusts and the like. Insurers have also funded mortgages for commercial borrowers and developers, who in turn use the money to build commercial centers, shopping centers, apartments, warehouses and houses.

The insurance industry is part of the larger financial services industry, which includes banks, brokerages, mutual funds, credit unions, trust companies, pension funds and similar organizations. Traditional barriers between industries have disappeared in part. Mutual funds can be sold by insurance companies and banks. Equities brokers handle cash management accounts. Banks have become active sellers of life insurance and annuities and other insurance products. Insurers themselves have developed products that include savings, protection and investment elements.

How Insurance Is Sold

Insurance is sold through a variety of channels, including face-to-face by insurance agents and brokers, over the internet, through the mail, by phone, in workplace programs and through associations and affinity groups.

Insurance agents generally represent the insurance company. Insurance brokers usually represent the insured client but can sometimes act as an insurance agent.

The insurance agent (or producer) can be a key component in the underwriting process by taking the role of intermediary.

Unlike the underwriter, the agent is positioned to meet with the applicant, ask pertinent questions and gauge responses. Information gathered from the interview may become the basis the underwriter uses in decision making. As a benefit to the consumer, many agents—called independent agents—represent several insurance companies, and may have a better view of each company's risk-selection threshold.

CHAPTER 1: INDUSTRY OVERVIEW

A "captive" or "tied" agent works primarily with a single insurer or a group of insurers, and may receive business leads or some sort of special preference for having that relationship. The insurer often offers benefits, such as health coverage, marketing support and training to the captive agent.

Generally speaking, insurance companies with a captive agent force also may see better policyholder retention. For starters, independent agents are less likely to follow policyholders from one state to another when they move; many independent agents are not licensed in multiple states. Larger insurance organizations may have the resources to track and follow an insured, and they may alert a new agent in the area to where the policyholder has moved.

In addition to agents, the following channels are used to get the business of insurance done:

Brokers: These producers do not necessarily work for an insurance company. Instead, the broker will place policies for clients with the carrier offering the most appropriate rate and coverage terms. The broker is rewarded by the carrier, often at a rate that differs than that paid to the carrier's agents.

Managing General Agents: These individuals or organizations are granted the authority by an insurer to perform a wide array of functions that can include placing business and issuing policies.

Agents are paid commissions based on the value and type of products they sell. Some insurers pay brokers additional compensation based on how the business performs.

Direct Sales: Direct selling of insurance to consumers through mail, internet or telephone solicitations has exploded in recent years. Insurance companies can bypass commissions by removing the agent from the transaction, although marketing and other associated costs can offset the savings.

Increasingly, online relationships are facilitated by traffic aggregators—basically

Best's Rankings
Top 20 Global Brokers - 2021 Edition
Ranked by 2020 Total Revenue

2020 Ranking	2019 Ranking	Broker	2020 Total Revenue
1	1	Marsh McLennan	$17.20 billion
2	2	Aon plc	$11.07 billion
3	3	Willis Towers Watson	$9.35 billion
4	4	Arthur J. Gallagher & Co.	$6.00 billion
5	5	Hub International	$2.70 billion
6	6	Brown & Brown Inc.	$2.61 billion
7	7	Truist Insurance Holdings Inc.	$2.44 billion
8	8	Lockton Inc.	$2.10 billion
9	9	Acrisure LLC	$2.04 billion
10	10	USI Insurance Services LLC	$1.98 billion
11	11	Alliant Insurance Services Inc.	$1.80 billion
12	13	AssuredPartners Inc.	$1.71 billion
13	12	NFP Corp.	$1.60 billion
14	14	Amwins Group Inc.	$1.50 billion
15	16	Howden Group Holdings*	$991.0 million
16	17	The Ardonagh Group	$973.4 million
17	15	CBIZ Inc.	$963.9 million
18	18	EPIC Insurance Brokers & Consultants	$725.5 million
19	n/a	Confie	$507.3 million
20	20	Fanhua Inc.	$500.9 million

*Formerly Hyperion Insurance Group

an alternative term for price-comparison sites. The aggregator service links the consumer to the insurer. Aggregator companies receive a commission from product providers when a policy is sold. They also may charge a fee based on any click-through to those providers.

The aggregator service can present challenges on two fronts: The site encourages consumers to select insurance policies based almost exclusively on price, and direct sales are a threat to the independent agent.

Important Functions of Insurance Organizations

Investment: Insurers look to investment managers to make sure they have the funds available to pay claims in a timely manner, match expected losses with investments that mature or become available at appropriate times and help generate income that will contribute to profits. Investment professionals handling insurance assets have an additional complication: Insurers are prohibited by state regulators from investing too heavily in riskier, more volatile instruments. For that reason most insurers are heavily weighted in bonds and similar instruments, and less heavily invested in stocks.

Actuarial: Insurance is based on probability and statistics. Actuaries are skilled in both areas and use their training to help insurers set rates, develop and price policies and coverage, determine reserves for anticipated claims and develop new products that provide coverage at a profit. Actuaries must pass extensive exams to earn their formal designations. Actuaries play influential roles in all sectors of insurance, including property/casualty, life, health and reinsurance. The role of actuaries grows as noninsurance industries—such as hedge funds, risk modelers and capital markets participants—become involved in developing risk products and programs.

Underwriting: At the heart of insurance is the art and science of assuming risk. Underwriters use a combination of data gathering and analysis, interviewing and professional knowledge to evaluate whether a given risk meets the insurer's standards for prudent evaluation. Their job is to evaluate whether given risks can be covered and, if so, under what terms. Underwriting departments often have the authority to accept or reject risks. Perhaps the most significant responsibility of underwriters is to determine premium that recognizes the likelihood of a claim and enables the insurer to earn a profit. Some of the process has been automated, such as when auto and homeowners insurers access information like driving and property records. Applicants for life insurance and some forms of health coverage may be asked to obtain medical evaluations.

Claims: Sometimes called the actual "product" that insurance companies deliver, claims departments usually operate in two areas: at the offices of the insurer and

CHAPTER 1: INDUSTRY OVERVIEW

Best's Rankings
World's Largest Insurance Companies – 2021 Edition
Based on 2019 net non-banking assets.

2019 Asset Rank	2018 Asset Rank	AMB#	Company Name	Country of Domicile	2019 Net Non-Banking Assets US$ (000)	% Change*
1	2	085014	Allianz SE	Germany	1,096,870,880	12.75
2	3	058182	Prudential Financial, Inc.	United States	896,552,000	10.00
3	1	085085	AXA S.A.	France	843,323,040	-14.78
4	5	058334	Berkshire Hathaway Inc.	United States	817,729,000	15.53
5	4	090826	Nippon Life Insurance Company	Japan	742,784,884	1.61
6	6	058175	MetLife, Inc.	United States	740,463,000	7.70
7	9	086120	Legal & General Group Plc	United Kingdom	735,409,869	13.82
8	10	086446	Ping An Ins (Group) Co of China Ltd	China	708,648,924	16.08
9	7	090527	Japan Post Insurance Co., Ltd.	Japan	664,719,463	-3.03
10	12	052446	China Life Insurance (Group) Company	China	646,493,671	13.36
11	13	066866	Manulife Financial Corporation	Canada	619,267,646	7.85
12	14	085909	Aviva plc	United Kingdom	603,489,008	7.11
13	11	085124	Assicurazioni Generali S.p.A.	Italy	576,322,880	-0.24
14	16	046417	Dai-ichi Life Holdings, Inc.	Japan	556,635,296	7.28
15	15	090906	National Mut Ins Fed Agricultural Coop	Japan	535,522,083	-1.60
16	17	058702	American International Group, Inc.	United States	525,064,000	6.72
17	19	085244	Aegon N.V.	Netherlands	494,057,760	12.24
18	18	086056	CNP Assurances	France	493,210,256	5.98
19	21	093310	Credit Agricole Assurances	France	476,487,200	11.22
20	8	085925	Prudential plc	United Kingdom	454,214,000	-29.88
21	20	085485	Life Insurance Corporation of India	India	426,706,202	3.07
22	22	086976	Zurich Insurance Group Ltd	Switzerland	404,688,000	2.36
23	23	090828	Meiji Yasuda Life Insurance Company	Japan	395,260,931	1.17
24	25	061691	New York Life Insurance Company	United States	371,648,000	9.58
25	24	091242	Sumitomo Life Insurance Company	Japan	358,420,471	2.20

* Percent change is based upon local currency. Source: BESTLINK

Best's Rankings
World's Largest Insurance Companies – 2021 Edition
Based on 2019 net premiums written.

2019 Premium Rank	2018 Premium Rank	AMB#	Company Name	Country of Domicile	2019 Net Premiums Written US$ (000)	% Change*
1	1	058106	UnitedHealth Group Incorporated[1]	United States	189,699,000	6.52
2	3	086446	Ping An Ins (Group) Co of China Ltd	China	110,746,845	10.51
3	2	085085	AXA S.A.	France	101,144,960	0.34
4	4	052446	China Life Insurance (Group) Company	China	97,744,867	7.52
5	5	070936	Kaiser Foundation Group of Health Plans	United States	97,247,349	5.64
6	6	058180	Anthem, Inc.	United States	94,730,000	11.38
7	7	085014	Allianz SE	Germany	86,656,640	6.45
8	10	085320	People's Ins Co (Group) of China Ltd	China	74,419,774	10.86
9	8	085124	Assicurazioni Generali S.p.A.	Italy	74,238,080	4.49
10	12	051149	Centene Corporation[1]	United States	71,714,000	25.13
11	9	020013	State Farm Group[2]	United States	70,640,883	-0.56
12	13	058052	Humana Inc[1]	United States	62,948,000	14.57
13	11	058334	Berkshire Hathaway Inc.	United States	62,811,000	6.07
14	15	086577	Munich Reinsurance Company	Germany	54,663,840	4.49
15	14	090826	Nippon Life Insurance Company	Japan	52,112,815	-6.75
16	19	070080	CVS Health Corp Group[2]	United States	52,026,207	13.57
17	17	085485	Life Insurance Corporation of India	India	50,491,133	12.42
18	21	090598	China Pacific Insurance (Group) Co Ltd	China	46,543,259	6.84
19	18	046417	Dai-ichi Life Holdings, Inc.	Japan	45,314,104	-8.58
20	20	085925	Prudential plc	United Kingdom	43,481,000	-2.14
21	16	090906	National Mut Ins Fed Agricultural Coop	Japan	42,580,588	-17.62
22	22	058175	MetLife, Inc.	United States	42,235,000	-3.66
23	23	086976	Zurich Insurance Group Ltd	Switzerland	41,251,000	0.05
24	26	093310	Credit Agricole Assurances	France	40,580,960	10.23
25	25	069154	Health Care Service Corporation Group	United States	40,052,991	5.27

* Percent change is based upon local currency. [1] Premiums shown are earned premiums. [2] AM Best consolidation; U.S. companies only. Source: BESTLINK

in the field through claims adjusters. Claims are requests for payment based on losses believed by the policyholder to be covered under an insurance policy. Claims personnel evaluate the request and determine the amount of loss the insurer should pay. Requests for claims payment can come directly to insurers or be handled by agents and brokers working directly with the insured. Claims adjusters can work directly for an insurer or operate as independent businesses that can work for multiple insurers. Claims adjusters often have designated levels of authority to settle claims. Adjusters serve as claims investigators and sometimes conduct elaborate investigations in the event of suspected fraudulent claims.

Insurance Entities

Ownership of traditional insurance companies generally comes in two structures, mutual and stock, although insuring entities may take a number of other forms, including reciprocal exchanges and risk retention groups. Mutual insurers are owned by and run for the benefit of their policyholders. Relative to insurance companies with shareholder ownership, mutual insurers have less access to the capital markets to raise money. Many mutual insurance companies have been formed by people or businesses with a common need, such as farmers. Mutuals pay a return of premium or "policyholder dividend" back to the policyholder if the company has strong financial results and a lower-than-expected level of claims. Policyholders also have the ability to vote on company leadership and have a say in certain corporate governance issues.

Best's Rankings
Top 10 U.S. Holding Companies - 2021 Edition
Ranked by Assets

Rank	Company Name	AMB#	2020 Total Assets ($000)	2019 Total Assets ($000)	% Change
1	Prudential Financial, Inc.	058182	940,722,000	896,552,000	4.90%
2	Berkshire Hathaway Inc.	058334	873,729,000	817,729,000	6.80%
3	MetLife, Inc.	058175	795,146,000	740,463,000	7.40%
4	American International Group, Inc.	058702	586,481,000	525,064,000	11.70%
5	Lincoln National Corporation	058709	365,948,000	334,761,000	9.30%
6	Principal Financial Group, Inc.	058179	296,627,700	276,087,800	7.40%
7	Equitable Holdings, Inc.	051409	275,397,000	249,818,000	10.20%
8	Brighthouse Financial, Inc.	046498	247,869,000	227,259,000	9.10%
9	UnitedHealth Group Incorporated	058106	197,289,000	173,889,000	13.50%
10	Pacific Mutual Holding Company	050799	190,672,000	171,473,000	11.20%

Ranked by Revenue

Rank	Company Name	AMB#	2020 Total Revenue ($000)	2019 Total Revenue ($000)	% Change
1	Berkshire Hathaway Inc.	058334	286,415,000	327,223,000	-12.50%
2	UnitedHealth Group Incorporated	058106	257,141,000	242,155,000	6.20%
3	Anthem, Inc.	058180	121,867,000	104,213,000	16.90%
4	Centene Corporation	051149	111,595,000	75,082,000	48.60%
5	Humana Inc.	058052	77,155,000	65,394,000	18.00%
6	MetLife, Inc.	058175	67,842,000	69,620,000	-2.60%
7	Prudential Financial, Inc.	058182	57,116,000	65,393,000	-12.70%
8	The Allstate Corporation	058312	44,795,000	44,681,000	0.30%
9	Liberty Mutual Holding Company Inc.	051114	43,796,000	43,228,000	1.30%
10	American International Group, Inc.	058702	43,736,000	49,746,000	-12.10%

Source: BESTLINK Holding Companies database

CHAPTER 1: INDUSTRY OVERVIEW

Reciprocal insurance companies resemble mutual companies. Whereas a mutual insurance company is incorporated, the reciprocal company is run by a management company, referred to as an attorney-in-fact.

Many mutuals were able to grow during the credit crunch of the late 2000s. Their growth is limited, however, because capital has to be generated internally, as there are no shares to sell. Some top former mutual insurance companies, including Metropolitan Life and Prudential, have demutualized to become shareholder-owned public companies. Typically, demutualization is done to raise capital or expand operations. Other companies, including Pacific Life and Liberty Mutual, took an intermediate step and became part of a mutual holding company structure.

A holding company structure, employed primarily in the United States, provides easier access to the capital markets, whereby shares can be sold to help raise capital. The holding company owns a significant amount, if not all, of another company's or other companies' common stock. Many insurance companies are part of a holding company structure, with the publicly traded parent company owning stock of the subsidiary or the controlled insurance company or companies.

Captive insurance companies are formed to insure the risks of their parent group or groups, and sometimes will insure risks of the group's customers. Captive insurers have become more high profile in recent years after many U.S. states and some international jurisdictions adopted legislation and rules encouraging captives to locate in their domiciles.

A risk retention group is a liability insurance company owned by its policyholders. Membership is limited to people in the same business or activity, which exposes them to similar liability risks. The purpose is to assume and spread liability exposure to group members and to provide an alternative risk financing mechanism for liability. These entities are formed under the Liability Risk Retention Act of 1986.

Structural differences between stock and mutual insurance companies affect business decisions. Stock companies have to answer to owners and policyholders, so if management's investment strategies are carried out with shareholder expectations in mind—seizing opportunities for growth and profit—they may be acting at the expense of policyholders. Mutuals, on the other hand, are owned by the policyholders, so the focus likely will be on affordability and dividends.

Observers have struggled to make meaningful comparisons of profitability generated by public and mutual companies. One thing is certain, however: No particular organizational structure is a cure-all for poorly conceived or executed strategies.

SPOTLIGHT

On High Alert: Rising Risks of PFAS Claims and Litigation Capture New Attention

Some industry experts are seeing parallels between PFAS risk and asbestos litigation that for years hit insurers hard. Insurers are now reacting by creating stand-alone products and adding PFAS-related policy exclusions for losses stemming from drinking water contamination, environmental remediation, and products liability and bodily injury claims related to the "forever chemicals."

In December 2020, 11 local water districts in California filed a lawsuit in Orange County Court alleging that four PFAS manufacturers—DuPont de Nemours, The Chemours Company, 3M and Corteva, along with roofing products manufacturer Decra Roofing Systems—were responsible for potentially more than $1 billion in cleanup and decontamination costs related to PFAS chemicals leaching into the districts' groundwater and water systems.

It wasn't the first time the companies have been brought into litigation over the use of the synthetic chemicals. In 2017, DuPont and its spinoff Chemours reached a $671 million settlement in roughly 3,550 personal injury lawsuits brought by citizens alleging they suffered health consequences from drinking water contaminated by chemical releases from a Parkersburg, West Virginia plant. The following year, 3M settled with Minnesota for $850 million for contaminating groundwater with chemicals used in its Scotchgard products.

PFAS, dubbed "forever chemicals" because of their pervasiveness and inability to break down in the environment for decades or even centuries, have long been used in many personal, household and commercial products. Along with environmental concerns, the man-made chemicals—of which there are more than 7,000 compounds—pose a potential threat to humans and have been linked to health risks such as reproductive and endocrine development disorders, certain types of cancer, and liver and immunological issues.

Much like in the early days of lawsuits targeting companies manufacturing or binding asbestos fibers and other products containing large quantities of the carcinogenic fibrous silicate mineral, and the staggering impact those claims had on liability insurance—a legacy that still haunts insurers today, "we're now seeing that once again with PFAS manufacturers," said attorney and shareholder John Gardella of the law firm CMBG3 Law LLC.

John Gardella

www.ambest.com

SPOTLIGHT

U.S. property/casualty insurers have been hard hit by asbestos and environmental losses over the years, and in the past five years alone paid out $16.1 billion for claims while incurring $11.3 billion in losses, according to a 2020 Best's Market Segment Report, *AM Best's A&E Loss Estimates Remain Unchanged.*

So far, the wave of PFAS lawsuits—many of which have also resulted in costly losses and settlements—has largely centered on environmental cleanup and remediation. But Gardella said lurking on the not-so-distant horizon is the growing threat of PFAS-related products liability and personal injury cases that could also significantly impact insurers and their bottom lines.

PFAS were accidentally developed by chemists in the late-1930s, and over the years the oil- and moisture-resistant chemicals were widely used in the production of everyday products such as nonstick cookware, water-repellent clothing, cosmetics, stain-resistant fabrics and carpets, aqueous firefighting foam and food packaging.

While the manufacturing and use of two specific PFAS compounds—perfluorooctanesulfonic acid (PFOS) and perfluorooctanoic acid (PFOA)—were phased out of the U.S. nearly 20 years ago, PFAS still pose a significant threat in the nation due to their environmental persistence and continued use or import in many consumer-based products such as food wrappers and furniture protectants, said Jamie Langes, assistant vice president of Philadelphia Insurance Companies' Midwest territory environmental division.

— Lori Chordas

Insurers Turn to Apprenticeships

Al Crook, head of HR business partners and apprenticeship at Zurich North America, years ago came across a troubling factoid: Some roles within the insurance industry ranked just behind those in real estate and the clergy in terms of age of employees.

He's quick to concede the apprenticeship program he helped found five years ago at Zurich isn't a panacea, but it was a good start that quickly grew into the multi-employer Chicago Apprentice Network. The enticements of Zurich's two-year program? Free education, a guaranteed job and a promotion following completion.

The goal is to look beyond college graduates, particularly those with insurance-related degrees, as the sole group of prospective employees.

"We knew that there was a model that worked in our European counterparts, and in other parts of the world apprenticeships are very popular," Crook said. "With the need to always have more talent and access to more talent, apprenticeships were an untapped and undeveloped source for that talent. We knew that we could build it so that it could be more popular both in the industry and across the region in which we work."

The federal Labor Department has made growing and expanding

apprenticeship a priority, launching "Discover Apprenticeship" five years ago as part of a larger effort to increase job training and add 1 million new apprentices by Sept. 30, 2021. Since Jan. 1, 2017, more than 800,000 people in the U.S. have found employment through apprenticeships, according to department figures. More than 9 in 10 workers who complete an apprenticeship earn an average of $70,000 a year, and 94% are still employed six months after program completion.

The Chicago Apprentice Network was launched in collaboration with Aon and Accenture and has grown from an inaugural class of 25 apprentices to 740 apprentices working with more than 40 employers across industries, according to Aon and the Chicago Apprentice Network. Crook said 116 people have been hired at Zurich through the program.

Zurich North America is part of Zurich Insurance Group, a multiline insurer founded in 1872, with about 54,000 employees today. The company provides a range of property/casualty and life insurance products and operates in more than 210 countries and territories.

Wider Net

Zurich North America's apprenticeship program is designed to broaden the company's employee base, but there are some hurdles to overcome.

"Over time, we fall in love with certain things. We've fallen in love with owning a car. We've fallen in love with owning a home. I believe as a country we also fell in love with the four-year degree," Crook said. "I think that's why other options like apprenticeships fell out of favor."

Zurich's earn-while-you-learn program—launched at its Schaumburg, Illinois, headquarters in 2016—provides a debt-free path to a professional career. Apprentices include high school graduates, veterans, those reentering the workforce after a hiatus, people wanting to move from a job to a career, and others attracted by the prospect of a guaranteed job and promotion.

As a rule, apprentices spend part of the week at work, and the rest at school. They receive pay, commensurate with an entry-level job, from sponsoring companies.

As Bridget Gainer, Aon's chief commercial officer, tells it, it's all about creating networks. Once a quarter, the Chicago Apprentice Network holds meetings—which she likens to speed dating—for apprentices, interns and prospective employers to connect. The events usually attract about 400 people and allow both newcomers and seasoned professionals to establish a base of mutual support, she said.

—Terrence Dopp

Al Crook

CHAPTER 2: PROPERTY/CASUALTY

Property/Casualty Market at a Glance

Property/casualty is known as "nonlife" insurance in many parts of the world. The word "property" usually refers to physical things, including autos, buildings, ships and other concrete items that can be lost, damaged or otherwise become a financial loss to the insured. The word "casualty" usually refers to the concept of liability, and is often associated with coverage of negligent acts or omissions. Casualty areas are some of the largest, including auto liability, professional liability, workers' compensation and general liability. The relative size of property/casualty insurers is often gauged by premiums collected.

In the United States, property/casualty insurers file a special statement with the National Association of Insurance Commissioners. The filing is designed to determine premiums and losses by lines of business and to give an accurate view of the insurer's reserving for loss.

As of this publication, AM Best's database contained filing statements for 5,528 total single companies operating in the U.S. property/casualty market. According to the U.S. Department of Labor, 557,400 people work in the property/casualty industry.

US Property Casualty - Top Insurers by Net Premiums Written (2020)
(US$ Billions)

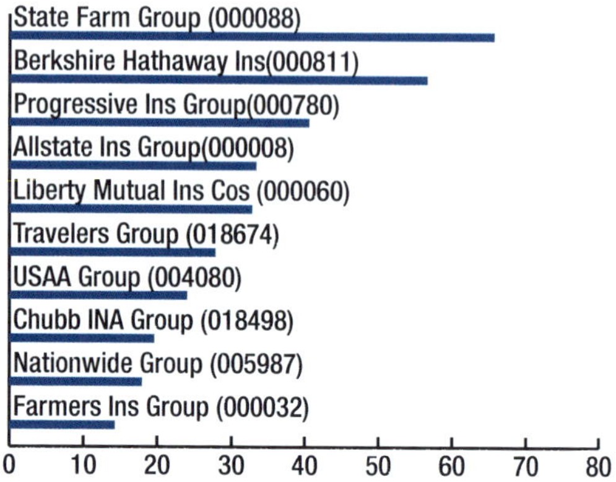

- State Farm Group (000088)
- Berkshire Hathaway Ins(000811)
- Progressive Ins Group(000780)
- Allstate Ins Group(000008)
- Liberty Mutual Ins Cos (000060)
- Travelers Group (018674)
- USAA Group (004080)
- Chubb INA Group (018498)
- Nationwide Group (005987)
- Farmers Ins Group (000032)

Source: BESTLINK – Aggregates & Averages Property/Casualty United States & Canada, 2021 Edition

US Property Casualty - Top Insurers by Gross Premiums Written (2020)
(US$ Billions)

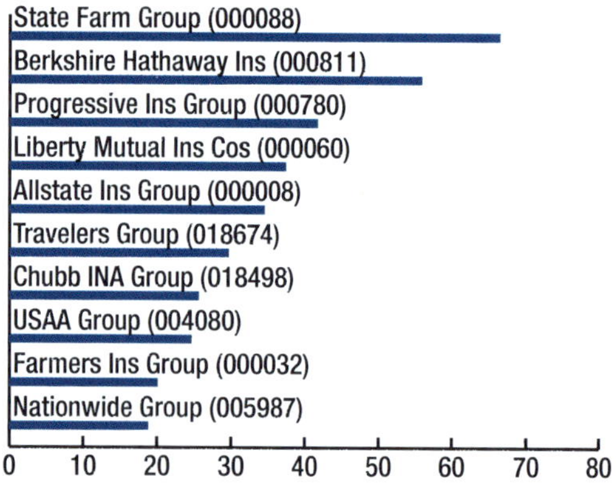

- State Farm Group (000088)
- Berkshire Hathaway Ins (000811)
- Progressive Ins Group (000780)
- Liberty Mutual Ins Cos (000060)
- Allstate Ins Group (000008)
- Travelers Group (018674)
- Chubb INA Group (018498)
- USAA Group (004080)
- Farmers Ins Group (000032)
- Nationwide Group (005987)

Source: BESTLINK – Aggregates & Averages Property/Casualty United States & Canada, 2021 Edition

According to AM Best's 2020 Review & Preview report, the property/casualty industry faces a range of issues.

AM Best believes that the trends affecting the results of the commercial lines before the pandemic are likely to remain headwinds in 2021. Among the issues the industry faces is the ongoing growth in social inflation, driven by emerging social trends and an increase in third-party litigation financing; rising reinsurance costs; and challenges associated with secondary catastrophe events, such as wildfires and convective storms. Additionally, with favorable pricing conditions expected to continue, companies without legacy concerns may have an opportunity to take advantage of those positive trends, increasing competition, and potentially short-circuiting price recovery. The current investment market is also a potential

CHAPTER 2: PROPERTY/CASUALTY

drag on operating performance, but it does drive a greater commitment to maintaining underwriting and pricing discipline to achieve desired total returns.

Surplus levels continue to support the underlying risks for most U.S. homeowners' carriers despite the adverse effects of more frequent catastrophes, the COVID-19 pandemic, and ongoing volatility in investments. Owing to the rebound in the equity markets throughout 2020, a vast majority of homeowners carriers were able to absorb the downturn with favorable risk-adjusted capitalization maintained. Additionally, core results remain profitable despite increased non-CAT weather losses and higher frequency of fire and water losses, owing to proactive underwriting actions, including improved pricing sophistication, ongoing exposure management, and diversified reinsurance programs. Advances in predictive modeling and pricing analytics, as well as third-party data, have provided opportunities for homeowners carriers to pursue profitable growth.

Key countervailing factors include elevated catastrophe activity, the rise in reinsurance pricing, and the ongoing economic impact of COVID-19. U.S. catastrophe losses trended well above normal levels in 2020, and are likely to remain moderately elevated, which will further fuel the rise in reinsurance pricing expected for 2021. Although the pandemic is not expected to materially affect the U.S. homeowners segment, ongoing depressed economic conditions and the inherent risk of price inflation for construction supplies and contractors may further increase the cost of adjusting claims, transporting goods, and labor.

Most personal auto writers maintain a consistently favorable capital position built upon ongoing use of newer technology and data analytics to supplement underwriting, claims handling and ratemaking. AM Best believes that the private passenger auto industry's favorable overall operating performance in recent years will continue throughout the remainder of 2021, owing to the improvement in auto claims frequency that has somewhat negated ongoing severity pressures. Frequency will continue to benefit from fewer drivers on the road for the foreseeable future, as the pandemic persists and employers extend

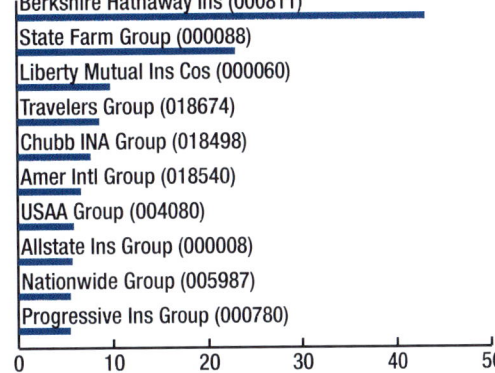

US Property Casualty - Top Insurers by Total Admitted Assets (2020)
(US$ Billions)

Source: BESTLINK – Aggregates & Averages Property/Casualty United States & Canada, 2021 Edition

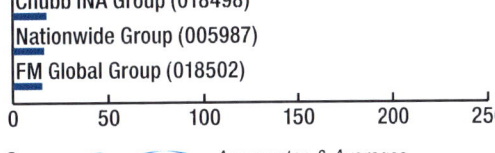

U.S. Property/Casualty – Policyholders' Surplus (2020)
(US$ Billions)

Source: BESTLINK – Aggregates & Averages Property/Casualty United States & Canada, 2021 Edition

CHAPTER 2: PROPERTY/CASUALTY

work-from-home operations or support hybrid work environments. Innovation in all operational phases and in risk management will also continue to benefit personal auto writers as they maintain their focus on pricing adequacy and auto repair management in order to remain competitive.

The main counterbalancing factors include the near- and medium-term economic fallout and market disruption arising from the pandemic, regulatory uncertainty, as well as the prevailing low interest rate environment, which will continue to pressure overall investment returns in 2021. However, given the compulsory nature of personal auto insurance, the effects of the pandemic on the segment appear to be more muted than on some of the commercial lines.

Property/Casualty Coverage Types and Lines of Business

Property insurance covers damages or loss of property. As a result, rates can be significantly higher in areas susceptible to perils such as hurricanes. Casualty insurance covers indemnity losses and legal expenses from losses such as bodily injury or damage that the policyholder may cause to others.

When a loss occurs, insurance companies establish a claim reserve for the amount of the expected cost of the claim using a projection of estimated loss costs over a period of time. While property reserves are established when a property loss occurs and are usually settled soon after a loss, casualty reserves are established for losses that may not be paid or settled for years (i.e. medical professional liability, workers' compensation, production liability and environmental-related claims). These "long-tail" lines of business are so named because of the length of time that may elapse before claims are finally settled.

Determining and comparing profitability among property/casualty companies typically is achieved through the combined ratio, which measures the percentage of claims and expenses incurred relative to premiums earned/written. A combined ratio of less than 100 means that the insurer is making an underwriting profit. Companies with combined ratios over 100 still may earn an operating profit, however, because the ratio does not account for investment income.

Property/casualty insurance generally falls into two areas of concentration: personal and commercial lines.

The two largest product lines within the personal lines sector are auto insurance and homeowners insurance.

Commercial lines include insurance for businesses, professionals and commercial establishments. There are many more varieties of commercial lines products than personal lines. The largest two lines are workers' compensation and other liability.

Personal Lines of Business

Personal insurance protects families, individuals and their property, typically homes and vehicles, from loss and damage. Auto and homeowners coverage dominates mostly because of legal provisions that mandate coverage be obtained.

Auto: The largest line of business in the property/casualty sector is auto insurance. According to AM Best's BestLink database, the top 50 groups writing auto insurance captured 89.6% of the total market in 2020, or $264 billion of the $295 billion for all U.S. auto coverage. The largest writer of U.S. private passenger auto, and all auto coverage overall, remains State Farm Group.

Auto insurance includes collision, liability, comprehensive, personal injury protection and coverage in the event another motorist is uninsured or underinsured.

Homeowners: The second-largest line of personal property/casualty insurance is homeowners, representing $110 billion in direct premiums written for the U.S. property/casualty industry in 2020. Historically, the leading cause of U.S. insured catastrophe losses has been hurricanes and tropical storms, followed by severe thunderstorms and winter storms. The top 50 groups writing homeowners multiperil coverage represented 86.5% of the U.S. market for homeowners coverage, according to AM Best's BestLink database. The largest writer of homeowners multiperil coverage is also State Farm Group.

U.S. Property/Casualty – Direct Premiums Written by Line (2020)
(US$ 000)

Business Line	Direct Premiums Written
Private Passenger Auto Liability	$148,169,885
No-Fault	16,408,253
Other Liability	131,761,632
Homeowners Multiple Peril	110,520,134
Private Passenger Auto Physical Damage	101,966,129
Other Liability	88,196,138
Occurrence	55,149,217
Claims-Made	31,758,898
Excess Workers' Compensation	1,288,022
Workers' Compensation	51,162,012
Commercial Multiple Peril	46,515,114
Non-Liability	30,391,239
Liability	16,123,876
Commercial Auto Liability	34,997,640
No-Fault	835,123
Other Liability	34,162,517
Inland Marine	25,936,458
Fire	16,788,327
Allied	16,587,447
Mult Peril Crop	10,825,797
Comm Auto Phys Damage	10,981,139
Medical Professional Liability	10,144,216
Surety	6,932,850
Mortgage Guaranty	5,746,837
Farmowners Multiple Peril	4,738,558
Group Accident & Health	4,729,574
Earthquake	4,278,144
Product Liability	4,243,280
Ocean Marine	4,171,312
Warranty	3,401,030
Federal Flood	3,045,673
Other Accident & Health	2,333,905
Credit	2,326,005
Aircraft	2,210,034
Boiler and Machinery	2,158,196
Fidelity	1,324,962
Private Crop	1,115,706
Private Flood	735,094
Financial Guaranty	476,488
Burglary and Theft	454,677
International	46,088
Aggregate Write-ins	1,403,105
Total P/C Industry	728,661,954

Note: Data for some companies in this report has been received from the NAIC.
Reflects Grand Total (includes Canada and U.S. Territories)
Source: BESTLINK — State/Line (P/C Lines) - P/C, US; Data as of: June 11, 2021

CHAPTER 2: PROPERTY/CASUALTY

Commercial Lines of Business

Commercial insurance protects businesses, hospitals, governments, schools and other organizations from losses.

Two of the largest lines in the commercial segment are workers' compensation and general liability.

Workers' Compensation: Insurers on behalf of employers pay benefits regardless of who is to blame for a work-related injury or accident, unless the employee was negligent. In return, the employee gives up the right to sue.

General Liability: General liability insurance protects business owners (the "insured") from the risks of liabilities imposed by lawsuits and similar claims. Liability insurance is designed to offer its insureds specific protection against third-party insurance claims; in other words, payment is not typically made to the insured, but rather to someone suffering loss who is not a party to the insurance contract. In general, damages caused by intentional acts are not covered under general liability insurance policies. When a claim is made, the insurance carrier has the duty to defend the insured.

Other major lines of business in the property/casualty commercial sector include:

Aircraft (all perils): Aircraft coverage is often excluded under standard commercial general liability forms. Coverage for aircraft liability loss exposure can include hull (physical damage) and medical payments coverages.

Allied Lines: Coverage for loss of or damage to real or personal property by reason other than fire. Losses from wind and hail, water (sprinkler, flood, rain), civil disorder and damage by aircraft or vehicles are included.

Boiler and Machinery: Coverage for damage to boilers, pressure vessels and machinery.

Burglary and Theft: Coverage to protect property from burglary, theft, forgery, counterfeiting, fraud and the like. Protection can include on- and off-premises exposure.

Commercial Auto: Coverage that protects against financial loss because of legal liability for injury to persons or damage to property of others caused by the insured's commercial motor vehicle.

Commercial Multiple Peril: Commercial insurance coverage combining two or more property, liability and/or risk exposures.

Fidelity: Coverage for employee theft of money, securities or property, written with a per loss limit, a per employee limit or a per position limit. Employee dishonesty coverage is one of the key coverages provided in a commercial crime policy.

Financial Guaranty: Credit protection for investors in municipal bonds, commercial mortgage-backed securities and auto or student loans. Provides financial recourse in the event of a default on the bond or other instrument.

Fire: Coverage for loss of or damage to real or personal property due to fire or lightning. Losses from interruption of business and loss of other income from these sources are included.

Inland Marine: Coverage for goods in transit and goods, such as construction equipment, subject to frequent relocation.

Medical Professional Liability: Protects against failure to use due care and the standard of care expected from a doctor, dentist, nurse, hospital or other health-related organization.

Mortgage Guaranty: Insurance against financial loss because of nonpayment of principal, interest and other amounts agreed to be paid under the terms of a note, bond or other evidence of indebtedness that is secured by real estate.

Multiple Peril Crop: Protects against losses caused by crop yields that are too low. This line was developed initially by the U.S. Department of Agriculture.

Ocean Marine: Provides protection for all types of oceangoing vessels and their cargo as well as legal liability of owners and shippers.

Products Liability: Protection against loss arising out of legal liability because of injury or damage resulting from the use of a product or the liability of a contractor after a job is completed.

Surety: The surety bond guarantees that the principal of a bond will act in accordance with the terms established by the bond.

SPOTLIGHT

Strength Through Specialization

Creating new markets and products to meet the challenge of emerging risks is at the heart of the excess and surplus lines market.

The most difficult risks in the insurance industry often end up in the excess and surplus lines space.

Key to success in the E&S space are expertise and having the knowledge to write risks that the standard market shuns, said three leaders who've built their careers in the E&S market.

Those leaders—Steve DeCarlo, executive chairman, AmWINS Group; Pat Ryan, founder, chairman and chief executive officer, Ryan Specialty Group; and Matt Power, president, One80 Intermediaries—discussed successes and challenges in the E&S market.

Maintaining Focus

"Specialization is paramount when you talk about E&S," DeCarlo said. "You can't go out to a retail client and fake it. You have to be great at what you do. Retailers demand that we're great at what we do, and so do the markets, frankly. We were highly focused on making sure that how we came to market was at a level that proved our expertise."

Charlotte, N.C.-based AmWINS Group Inc., the largest independent wholesale distributor of specialty insurance products in the United States, operates through more than 115 offices globally and places $20 billion in annual premium.

DeCarlo served as chief executive officer of AmWINS for 17 years, leading the business through the merger of several specialty wholesalers, and has served on the AmWINS board of directors since he joined the company in December 2000.

"I think fundamentally, when we set out to build a foundation to the business and overall, when we thought about our strategy, what we'd set out to do was think about how to build a business that our retail clients and our market partners could look to, and how we could look to the next 150 years," DeCarlo said. "Without that structure, we wouldn't be successful."

One key to maintaining that focus was employee ownership, he said. More than 40% of AmWINS is owned by about 725 employee shareholders.

"Employee ownership was a critical thing that we focused on, and getting that aligned so that all our employees could feel that ownership meant a lot to us. We had to make sure that we'd focused on training

Steve DeCarlo

SPOTLIGHT

and making sure that we were experts at what we did," DeCarlo said.

DeCarlo said the company also focused on diversification. "We didn't want to be siloed as just great at Southeast wind, or just great at earthquake, or just great at casualty."

Pat Ryan, the founder and former chairman of Aon, launched Ryan Specialty Group in 2010. "It's a very competitive business," Ryan said. "It's a real value-add business; it's one that brings advice and advocacy to the retailer on behalf of their clients. When we're the MGA, a market needs to become a go-to market. We only do underwriting, hopefully, where we can differentiate ourselves."

The strategy in building E&S business is specialization, Ryan said. He looks for the top intellectual capital in specialty lines, and focuses on attracting, retaining, empowering and supporting them.

"Then, we split it into verticals," Ryan said. Practice groups are formed based on industry and product. This can include both distribution wholesale brokers or managing general underwriters, he said. Ryan Specialty, like many others, has both.

"We find that focusing with experts on an industry and a product really allows us to differentiate the talent," Ryan said. "Critically, we believe it's important to align our talent with the retail broker's talent in that same specialty line, and then take it to a market that also has the specialty talent, so that we have alignment from the insured being represented by the retailer, to the wholesaler and to the capital provider."

He emphasized the importance of innovation. "A broker always wants to be able to differentiate themselves from their competition, not on price but on form, on any kind of exclusive opportunity that they might have with the market," Ryan said.

Matt Power served as executive vice president for Lexington Insurance Co. before becoming president of One80 Intermediaries, which was formally launched in December 2019. During his tenure in the E&S market, Power watched the industry evolve.

"If you think about the E&S business 20 or 25 years ago, it was highly fragmented," Power said. The E&S market had businesses based in individual cities, and they specialized in either property or casualty. During dramatic market cycles, business was feast or famine.

Which was why "this notion of building diversity, uncorrelated cash flows, has been critically important to me," Power said.

—Staff

Patrick Ryan

SPOTLIGHT

Independent Streak

In a conference call to analysts, Allstate Chair, President and CEO Tom Wilson outlined the company's transformative growth plan that included an overhaul of how the insurer conducts business.

Part of the revitalization plan, Wilson said, recognizes customers' changing needs, largely driven by increased connectivity and advanced analytics.

But while customers are becoming more comfortable with digital approaches and self-service, Wilson said they still prefer agents when purchasing a policy.

Allstate is heeding that call and growing its existing independent agency force by adding relationships with 42,300 domestic agents through its acquisition of National General Holdings Corp.

Like many of its personal auto insurance peers, Allstate uses independent agents as part of its distribution mix, which includes a large captive agency force. Last year, 6% of the company's personal lines business was written by independent agents.

For decades insurers have used agents and brokers as their primary channel of distribution. However, the rise of auto writers like Geico and Progressive, whose books of business include large direct-sales operations, has created a sizable alternative to the agent channel.

A glance at today's personal auto market, however, shows independent agents still play a key role in distribution, said Brian Sullivan, editor and publisher of the Auto Insurance Report and Property Insurance Report.

A large portion of the top 10 U.S. private passenger auto writers now rely solely or partially on independent agents to market and sell products. Over the years, some insurers in the line have bolstered their stake in the channel through consolidation. In 2008, Liberty Mutual grew its independent agency base to nearly 15,000 agencies with its $6.2 billion acquisition of Safeco.

Last year Nationwide, the eighth-largest personal auto writer based on 2019 direct premiums written, according to BestLink, announced its decision to fully immerse itself in the channel in an attempt to meet members' changing needs and to provide agents with longer-range growth potential.

Nationwide, which held roughly 7% of the overall independent agency market in 2019, completed a two-year journey to end its exclusive agent distribution channel and transition entirely to an independent

Tom Wilson

SPOTLIGHT

agency force across all books of business, including personal auto.

Events such as the COVID-19 pandemic highlight opportunities in the line, said Jeff Rommel, senior vice president of property/casualty sales and distribution at Nationwide.

"Distribution has to match customer expectations, and COVID is accelerating that in many ways by highlighting consumers' desire for fast, easy digital solutions and different options from multiple carriers, coupled with the advice and counsel of a trusted professional like independent agents," he said.

Making the Move

Recent insurance shopping numbers, however, tell a slightly different tale.

When much of the nation shut down during the early stages of the COVID pandemic, auto insurers that rely on exclusive agents saw higher shopping growth rates than independent agents and direct channels, ending the 2020 second quarter at 15% growth year-over-year for June, according to the latest LexisNexis Risk Solutions Insurance Demand Meter, which reports quarterly U.S. auto insurance shopping activity.

But those numbers aren't deterring companies like Nationwide from commiting to independent agency distribution and projecting continued sales growth from the channel.

This year, nearly 2,000 existing agents under the Nationwide brand completed their transition to the independent agency model, joining the more than 10,000 U.S. independent agents that already have relationships with the company.

Bob Rusbuldt, CEO of the Independent Insurance Agents & Brokers of America, has long predicted shifts favorable to the independent agent channel.

"For the last 25 years, I've been saying that one day there would be just two distribution channels in the U.S.—the direct channel and the independent agency system. Now there is example after example proving that out, including Nationwide's move to become fully independent and Allstate's purchase of National General," he said.

AM Best senior analyst Michael Venezia pins many of those moves on evolving consumer behavior.

"In today's mobile-centric, internet-driven world customers want choice, and being offered a quote from just one insurer doesn't provide them many options," he said.

"Maybe it's not the cheapest price, but consumers now are more interested in having available options. And that's where independent agents can really shine as service advisers," Venezia said.

Allstate's Wilson hopes the company's expanding independent agency force and its planned $4 billion investment to acquire National General will not only scale up Allstate's auto business but also make it a top 5 carrier in the independent agency distribution channel.

— Lori Chordas

CHAPTER 3: LIFE
Life Market at a Glance

Life/health insurers cover the risks of dying, offer retirement savings products and provide a variety of protections against disability, specific types of illness and more. As of this publication, AM Best's database contained annual filings for 1,954 single life/health companies operating in the United States. Life insurers often have longer investment and coverage horizons because retirement and mortality are often events that are decades away. The relative size of life/health insurers is often gauged by assets under management. Life insurers have increasingly embraced annuities and other forms of retirement savings, as sales of traditional life products have been flat or grown modestly and baby boomers transition into retirement.

The U.S. life/health industry recorded total premiums of $634 billion and $4.8 trillion in total cash and invested assets as of 2020, the most recent full year available. The largest lines of business as measured by premium income, in order, are individual annuities, group annuities and ordinary life. Other lines of business include supplemental contracts, credit life, group life, industrial life, group accident & health,

Best's Rankings

Top 10 U.S. Life/Health Companies
Ranked by 2020 direct premiums written.
(US$ 000)

Rank	Company Name	AMB#	DPW
1	UnitedHealth Life Companies	069973	57,229,458
2	MetLife Life Ins Companies	070192	40,094,288
3	Aetna Life Group	070202	37,812,399
4	New York Life Group	069714	37,704,528
5	Massachusetts Mutual Life Group	069702	33,145,580
6	Prudential of America Group	070189	32,985,895
7	Lincoln Finl Group	070351	28,260,363
8	Aegon USA Group	069707	24,239,207
9	Cigna Life Group	070173	21,927,354
10	John Hancock Life Insurance Group	069542	20,755,289

Top 10 U.S. Life/Health Companies
Ranked by 2020 net premiums written.
(US$ 000)

Rank	Company Name	AMB#	NPW
1	UnitedHealth Life Companies	069973	57,688,681
2	New York Life Group	069714	37,467,263
3	Prudential of America Group	070189	37,225,682
4	MetLife Life Ins Companies	070192	33,963,055
5	Aetna Life Group	070202	27,022,202
6	Lincoln Finl Group	070351	23,667,947
7	Aegon USA Group	069707	21,751,845
8	Cigna Life Group	070173	21,148,780
9	Northwestern Mutual Group	069515	19,148,804
10	Voya Finl Group	070153	17,743,961

Top 10 U.S. Life/Health Companies
Ranked by 2020 total admitted assets.
(US$ 000)

Rank	Company Name	AMB#	Total Admitted Assets
1	Prudential of America Group	070189	680,214,029
2	MetLife Life Ins Companies	070192	455,631,385
3	New York Life Group	069714	371,524,092
4	TIAA Group	070362	341,257,483
5	AIG Life & Retirement Group	070342	327,189,170
6	Lincoln Finl Group	070351	315,122,559
7	Massachusetts Mutual Life Group	069702	313,208,996
8	Northwestern Mutual Group	069515	308,865,152
9	John Hancock Life Insurance Group	069542	302,129,970
10	Jackson Natl Group	069578	297,086,121

Top 10 U.S. Life/Health Companies
Ranked by 2020 capital & surplus.
(US$ 000)

Rank	Company Name	AMB#	Capital & Surplus
1	TIAA Group	070362	40,001,277
2	Northwestern Mutual Group	069515	24,957,453
3	Massachusetts Mutual Life Group	069702	24,327,413
4	New York Life Group	069714	19,610,021
5	Prudential of America Group	070189	17,859,206
6	MetLife Life Ins Companies	070192	17,182,255
7	State Farm Life Group	070126	13,751,506
8	Pacific Life Group	069720	11,364,193
9	AIG Life & Retirement Group	070342	10,959,749
10	Thrivent Finl for Lutherans	006008	10,698,406

Source: BESTLINK AM Best data.

credit accident & health and other accident & health.

According to the 2021 edition of *Best's Key Rating Guide - Life/Health, United States and Canada*, Prudential of America Group leads the list of largest life/health groups and unaffiliated singles ranked by total admitted assets, with $680 billion in total admitted assets as of year-end 2020.

U.S. Life/Health – 2020 Asset Distribution

- Real estate $22,980,590
- Other investments $30,201,245
- *Stock $118,963,122
- Derivatives $121,695,446
- Contract loans $133,310,983
- Cash & short-term investments $156,976,439
- Other invested assets (Schedule BA) $235,511,625
- Mortgage loans $600,426,073
- *Total bonds $3,388,229,857

Source: BESTLINK *Aggregates & Averages Life/Health U.S. & Canada 2020 Edition.* Securities are reported on the basis prescribed by the National Association of Insurance Commissioners.

Risk Profile

The risk profile of life insurance is very different from that of property/casualty insurance. Life insurance is generally more asset-intensive, and most product liabilities have a substantially longer duration.

The main purpose of life insurance is to cover the risk of dying too early or, in the case of annuities, the risks that may come with living longer than expected. Policies help beneficiaries maintain their standard of living after the policyholder dies. They also can protect beneficiaries and insureds from the possibility of outliving their assets.

While some types of life insurance include a savings component that can provide retirement income, life insurance itself isn't necessarily an investment. But for insurance companies, and especially life insurers, profitability is largely dependent on investment performance. In general, life insurers have enough data surrounding life expectancies and risk classes to determine rates and to accurately predict claims.

Because a policy can remain in effect for decades, life insurers' obligations tend to be relatively long term. As a result, many insurers invest in longer-duration assets such as long-term bonds and real estate.

CHAPTER 3: LIFE

Life Insurers Chasing Wider Range of Opportunities

AM Best's annual Review & Preview report details a range of key trends shaping the future for life/annuity insurers.

Intense competition in the fixed-annuity space has also forced insurers to search for new distribution channels or to seek other avenues for growth. The influx into the market of direct-annuity writers backed by private equity offering generous crediting rates has put some pressure on more established companies. In addition, fixed-indexed annuities that offer guaranteed living benefit riders had in recent years become necessary for fixed-annuity writers to remain competitive.

Well-established insurers have focused more on growing the bank and broker/dealer channel, as they require a high rating, which many of the new entrants have not obtained. According to the Secure Retirement Institute, bank sales accounted for 41% of fixed-rate, deferred-annuity sales in the third quarter, up 85% from prior-year period. Some insurers that have established direct-to-consumer (DTC) distribution capabilities have experienced a noticeable increase in sales, although from a relatively low base, as the share of new business in the DTC channel has historically accounted for a modest amount of overall sales.

The increased DTC sales were also primarily for more simplified products—consumers would still rather speak with a live financial representative for more complex retirement-type products.

Given the stiff competition in the individual annuity segment, a growing number of insurers have identified the pension risk transfer (PRT) market as an area for potential growth. Although interest rates remain low and U.S. single-premium buyout sales declined 32% in the first nine months of 2020 from prior-year period (according to the Secure Retirement Institute), many medium-sized players feel that this product is a good fit for them as it can also provide a partial hedge to their mortality books of business. PRT has historically been dominated by a handful of large insurers, with the U.K. the most mature market, but many medium-sized U.S. companies are eyeing this growing market. They believe they have the capacity on their balance sheets to handle smaller to medium-sized transactions, perhaps partnering with a reinsurer on larger deals.

Company Business Profiles Being Reshaped by Low Interest Rates

Given the prolonged low-interest-rate environment, pressure continues to mount as insurers know the levers they can pull without worsening their company risk profiles. Spread compression and declining investment yields have been a concern for some time, and market volatility and uncertainty suggest the problem will only get worse, as guaranteed rates on many older blocks of business remain a burden for many insurers.

28

Insurers are under intense pressure to continue to cut expenses while investing in digital capabilities. Historically, insurers have been able to mitigate this pressure through new product pricing on the liability side of the balance sheet, including lowering cap rates for indexed products, scaling back pricing on variable annuity living benefit riders, and lowering crediting rates and dividend scales. For over a decade now, life/annuity insurers have been transitioning away from more volatile lines of business and have cut back or discontinued sales of universal life products with secondary guarantees, divested in-force legacy annuity blocks, and completely ceased sales of new variable annuities (VA) with living benefits. These actions have been further supported by ongoing expenses savings through automation and the elimination of redundant processes. As a result, insurers have generally been able to maintain target return ratios while unlocking some capital from insurance operations, which they have either returned to shareholders or used to support growing operations. However, many of those actions have also made these de-risked products less attractive to consumers and more difficult for insurance agents and financial representatives to sell.

AM Best observed a recalibration of priorities by innovation teams during 2020, which often included pausing major initiatives that weren't deemed essential to manage regulatory hurdles, direct competition, or general business continuity. Many innovative products have apparently been put on the back burner until macro-economic conditions improve or at least return to some semblance of the pre-COVID-19 world. Because of companies' temporary halt to ventures deemed to be higher risk, AM Best innovation scores are slightly lower than initial productions, prior to the release of the criteria.

Life/annuity organizations have made efforts to better analyze distribution channels down to the individual level, to determine where the best-quality business is being sourced from. Finally, those entities with capital substantial enough to do so continue to offer resources to startups and other growing insurtech firms in the hope that these third-party initiatives can be later integrated into their own operations.

Top U.S. Life Reinsurers by Individual Life Insurance in Force, 2020

Company Name	Total Individual Amount in Force ($000)
SCOR Life US Group	1,786,143,253
RGA Reinsurance Company	1,768,965,426
Swiss Re Life & Health America Inc.	1,481,914,440
Hannover Life Reassurance Co of America	1,245,679,229
Munich American Reassurance Company	1,105,635,553
Canada Life Assurance Company USB	264,441,103
General Re Life Corporation	229,470,124
Optimum Re Insurance Company	81,793,286
Wilton Reassurance Company	79,188,588
Employers Reassurance Corporation	78,786,178
PartnerRe Life Reinsurance Co of America	72,930,289
M Life Insurance Company	56,224,059

Source: AM Best data and research

Growth has been a challenge for some time—particularly in the middle market for individual life insurance products—but there may be a silver lining to what has otherwise been a long and drawn-out catastrophic event. In responding to the needs of both employees and distributors to work remotely, many companies have effectively accelerated certain aspects of their planned technology initiatives. In doing so, they may be better positioning themselves to grow and to take advantage of what appears

Important Lines of Life Business and Products

Life insurers market a variety of life products that range from simple to complex.

Total Life, In Force & Issued: The size of a life company can be measured by the face amount of its portfolio—that is, the amount of life insurance it has issued as well as the amount in force. In force is the total face amount of insurance outstanding at a point in time. Issued measures the face amount of policies an insurer has sold within a given time period.

Permanent Life: Permanent life provides death benefits and cash value in return for periodic payments. Cash surrender value, or nonforfeiture value, is the sum of money an insurance company will pay a policyholder who decides to cancel the policy before its expiration or before the policyholder's death. Over the long term, these products usually produce solid, sustainable profitability that is derived from adequate pricing, underwriting and investment returns. Permanent life products include whole life, universal life and variable universal life.

Whole Life: Whole life pays a death benefit and also accumulates a cash value. These have a high initial expense strain for the issuing company due to large first-year commissions to agents as a percentage of premiums. Over time, whole life provides an income stream to the company and the agent. It carries premium, death benefit and cash value guarantees that other products don't provide.

Universal Life: These are flexible premium policies that incorporate a savings element. The cash values that are accumulated are put into investments with the intention of earning more in interest. Those accumulations can be used to reduce later premiums or to build up the cash value. For companies offering this product, the premium payment flexibility adds an element of uncertainty, as does the potential for changing market conditions that can affect interest rates. The next generation of this product line, universal life with secondary guarantees, offers competitive rates while providing long-term premium and death benefit guarantees, regardless of actual performance. The tight pricing and high reserve requirements can limit profitability. Indexed universal life is now the most popular iteration of universal life.

Variable Universal Life: These flexible premium policies allow for investments of the cash value into mutual fund-like accounts the insurance carrier holds in separate accounts rather than in its general account. Because policy values will vary based on the performance of investments, these policies present an investment risk to the

policyholder. Rather than having a monthly addition to the cash value based on a declared interest-crediting rate, the accumulated cash value of the variable policy is adjusted daily to reflect the investment experience of the funds selected. Insurers can be susceptible to profit fluctuations because of the equity market's effect on mutual fund fees. In addition, the insurer lacks control over separate account assets, and policyholder behavior may impact profitability.

Term Life: Term life provides protection for a specified period of time. It pays a benefit only if the insured's death occurs during the coverage period. It can be considered a pure protection product and a consumer's entry-level life insurance product. Term periods typically range from one year to 30 years, although there are annually renewable policies, which are designed for longer durations. Term life, which is a highly competitive product, is marketed through many traditional distribution channels, as well as through financial institutions, banks and various direct distribution channels including the internet. More recent products offer long-term premium guarantees, where the premium is guaranteed to be the same for a given period of years. Return of premium (ROP) term products have also become popular of late, offering policyowners a refund of all premiums paid if the insured is still alive at the end of the term period. Concerns to insurers include high lapse rates, compressed margins and high reserve requirements.

Group Life: Generally in the form of term life, group life is marketed to employers or association groups. The cost also may be shared by the participant and the master policyholder, usually the employee and employer, respectively. Typically, an initial benefit level may be paid by the employer, and, in some cases, employees may elect to pay for additional coverage. As with term life, competition is intense.

Annuity Products

Insurance companies provide annuities, which, at their most basic, are contracts that ensure an income stream. A payment or series of payments is made to an insurance company, and in return, the insurer agrees to pay an income for a specified time period. Annuities can take many forms but have a couple of basic properties: an immediate or deferred payout with fixed (guaranteed) or variable returns. Consequently, different annuity types can resemble certificates of deposit, pensions or even investment portfolios.

Challenges to the Annuity Industry

Life insurance companies must minimize the risk of disintermediation. This happens when deferred annuity holders seeking higher-yielding alternatives withdraw funds prematurely (often during periods of increasing interest rates), and force companies to pay these surrenders by liquidating investments that may be in an unrealized loss position. Insurers can mitigate this risk by matching the duration of its interest-sensitive liability portfolio with the duration of its asset portfolio, and by selling a diversified portfolio of products. Insurers also mitigate risk by designing deferred annuities with market-value adjustments on surrender values.

Immediate Annuities: These annuities are designed to guarantee owners a pre-determined income stream on a monthly, quarterly, semiannual or annual basis in exchange for a lump sum. Options are limited from the annuity holder's perspective, so profits are generally less volatile in the short term. However, the long-term nature of these products exposes the insurer to reinvestment risk and longevity risk.

Group Annuities: These differ slightly from individual annuities in that the payout is dependent on the life expectancy of all the members of the group rather than on the individual. Many company retirement plans, such as 401(k) plans, are annuities that will pay a regular income to the retiree. Tax-deferred annuity plans—403(b) and 457 plans—utilize group annuities as the investment vehicle for participant contributions.

Deferred Annuities: Deferred annuities are a type of long-term savings product that allows assets to grow tax-deferred until annuitization. This product category includes:

Fixed-Deferred Annuities: These products guarantee a minimum rate of interest during the time the account is growing and typically guarantee a minimum benefit upon annuitization.

For the issuer, fixed annuities are subject to significant asset/liability mismatch risks, as described above. Also, when interest rates fall, spread earnings—or the difference between the yield on investments and credited rates—can decrease, and asset cash flows must be reinvested at lower rates.

Fixed-Indexed Annuities: These products are credited with a return that is based on changes in an equity index. The insurance company typically guarantees a minimum return. Payouts may be periodic or in a lump sum. The potential for gains is an attractive feature during favorable market conditions; however, gains may not be as favorable as those available from variable annuities or straight equity investments. Sales of these products may decline if equity markets go through a prolonged downturn or a prolonged upturn.

Variable Annuities: The participant is given a range of investment options, typically mutual funds, from which to choose. The rate of return on the purchase payment, and the amount of the periodic payments, will vary depending on the performance of the selected investments and the level of expense charges in the product.

Variable annuity sales tend to slump during unfavorable equity market conditions. In addition, the primary sources of revenue for these products are account value-based fees, which also decline when market conditions deteriorate. Relatively thin margins, increasing product complexity (e.g., guaranteed living benefits) and volatile capital

requirements put variable annuities at the riskier end of the product continuum, from the standpoint of the issuing insurer.

Because variable annuities allow for investments in equity and fixed-income securities, they are regulated by the U.S. Securities and Exchange Commission. Fixed annuities and fixed-indexed annuities are not securities and, as such, are not regulated by the SEC.

Registered Index-Linked Annuities: A hybrid between a variable annuity and a fixed-indexed annuity, these products offer somewhat more of an upside growth potential than traditional fixed-indexed annuities in exchange for a certain level of downside risk, although less than traditional variable annuities. As registered products, they can only be sold by FINRA-registered representatives.

Accident & Health Products

Credit Accident & Health: This insurance covers a borrower for accidental injury, disability and related health expenses. It is designed specifically to make monthly payments until the insured can recover and resume earning income. If an individual is totally disabled for the life of the loan, the policy would pay the remaining balance, in most cases, but only one month at a time.

Group Accident & Health: These plans are designed for a natural group, such as employees of a single employer, or union members, and their dependents. Insurance is provided under a single policy, with individual certificates issued to each participant.

Other Accident & Health: Products that fall into this category could be policies for individuals that cover major medical, disability insurance, long-term care, dental, dread disease or auxiliary coverages such as Medicare supplement.

CHAPTER 3: LIFE

Cryptocurrency: Insurance Industry Tests the Waters With New Initiatives

Across the insurance industry—from life insurance to property/casualty, auto insurers to brokers—companies are taking their first steps into the realm of cryptocurrencies as they gain wider acceptance among both private and institutional investors.

In some cases, that takes the form of letting customers pay premiums with digital coins, or it can mean paying claims with the currency when a driver gets in an accident.

It may also take the shape of investments and new business lines—as in institutions themselves putting money into the cryptocurrency market and insurers protecting so-called digital wallets against hacking or theft.

And there's the technology itself: The currencies are based on blockchains, which embed information at every step and offer new levels of claims processing and efficiency.

As digital currencies such as Bitcoin and Ethereum enter the mainstream, those in the industry like Benjamin Peach, who helps oversee digital assets for mega-brokerage Aon plc, want to try and get in on the action.

In the case of Aon, the professional service organization focused on risk, retirement and health has partnered with Nayms to build extra capacity and product offerings in the insurance market for digital asset risks.

Peach, associate director and digital assets specialist with the Global Broking Centre at Aon, said the end-goal is creating a platform in which crypto risks can be priced and underwritten in the digital currencies being insured.

"As more and more financial institutions are starting to adopt crypto as a payment service or even trading these currencies, then there is more of an onus for large players such as Aon within this space to cater to that demand," he said. "We need to make certain that we are servicing our clients to the best of our ability and part of that is developing and looking at new opportunities for transfer of risk."

At their root, cryptos are digital-based units of currency either used in lieu of traditional, government-backed fiat currencies like the U.S. dollar, or held as

Benjamin Peach

an investment like any foreign exchange currency.

There are several led by the likes of Bitcoin and Ethereum, and culling that to a front-runner is seen as one impediment to adoption.

A key difference from fiat currencies is that cryptos—a class of currencies sometimes referred to as "decentralized finance" due to lack of a central bank—exist in a purely digital realm. And there can be volatility: A Bitcoin's value dropped as much as 50% in June 2021 from its high of $60,000.

Peach said financial lines and the market for cyber insurance are natural first fits for a test run of crypto-based insurance.

"They're new lines of business when you look at the history of insurance products, which continuously need to innovate to keep up with industry demands," Peach said. "Both lines of businesses can offer comprehensive risk mitigation for a digital asset company." According to Gemini, a crypto exchange, an estimated 21.2 million U.S. adults, or roughly 14%, own some form of crypto, and there is demand for more.

Taking Steps

Metromile Inc., the pay-per-mile auto insurer whose entrance into the industry promised to meld technology and insurance, said it would begin a pilot program of allowing its customers to pay premiums and receive claims payouts in cryptocurrency. The company also bought $10 million in Bitcoin for its general accounts.

As more mature insurers look to work cryptocurrency into existing business models, Evertas—known as BlockRe until a February 2021 rebranding— is one example of a new company looking to build operations from the ground up. The firm will cover institutional holders of crypto assets and plans to focus initially on covering the theft of the private keys that underline ownership of a crypto asset. It has raised almost $5.8 million in seed funding.

J. Gdanski, founder and chief executive of Evertas, said the company partners with incumbent insurers and provides a "bridge" to a burgeoning part of the financial sector that's only going to grow in terms of assets and importance. The firm cites a lack of capacity as the biggest issue holding back the wider adoption of crypto.

"We are solving the last major infrastructure problem for the crypto industry which is a lack of insurance, and simultaneously we're pioneering the first new risk since cyber for the traditional insurance industry," Gdanski said. "You have incumbents who are ignoring something because they think it's too niche or too risky or not ready for prime time—none of which is correct at this point—and by the time they realize they want or need to address this market, it's too late."

Rick Chen, a Metromile spokesman, said the company's flagship offering was based around the idea of giving drivers more choice in the manner in which they secure coverage. Using Bitcoin and other cryptos is a response to

SPOTLIGHT

consumer demand and is an extension of that, he said.

While the company's pilot program had yet to begin taking any payments, he said initial indicators looked good and demand was growing. As a way to prove just how mainstream the once-fringe currency has become, he points to the inclusion of coins on U.S. tax forms.

Insurance companies have so far used blockchain technology to handle claims and operations, but the adoption of the actual currency is still a new frontier.

"We see ourselves as a digital insurance platform," he said. "We believe that supporting Bitcoin, or any cryptocurrency in this decentralized finance movement, is an extension of that—more choice. That's the primary reason we wanted to adopt this."

The underlying technology also offers insurers promise through things like potentially enabling smart contracts and claims handling on the Ethereum blockchain that will improve back-office functions, Chen said.

Metromile, unlike other insurers who have announced plans to accept payment in Bitcoin and then have it immediately converted to fiat currencies, will deal in crypto on its own book. Because the program is new, Chen said results aren't yet available.

"We plan to take your Bitcoin one-for-one," Chen said. "Eventually, we have it in a part of our store on our book and we can also then use that to make these claims payments in Bitcoin or, even in the future, other cryptocurrency."

For all of the volatility inherent in the class, there have also been many investors who have made a lot of money in decentralized finance through early investments that have paid multiples. The moves into the space are in many ways a chance for insurers to tap into that growth and let people spend a bit of those profits.

And in coming years, Peach said, individuals and consumers will have a choice: Either pay for goods and services through government-backed currencies that may well be on blockchain and cash free, or in a decentralized currency.

"Let's say you bought Ethereum in 2014. It's actually way more cost effective for you to part with a small amount of that in 20 years when it's at a much higher price," he said. "That's a nice problem to have."

—Terrence Dopp

Health Market at a Glance

Health insurers focus principally on providing health care coverage and related protection products. AM Best's database contains annual filing information for more than 1,300 single health insurance companies in the United States.

Health insurers typically have shorter investment horizons than life insurers or property/casualty insurers that focus on liability coverage. Health insurers are measured by premiums and membership in their programs, sometimes known as "covered lives."

The most recent report by the Kaiser Family Foundation estimates that about 49% of the U.S. population was covered by employer-sponsored health insurance. Another 21% was covered by Medicaid, a joint federal-and-state program for those of limited financial means. Another 14% of the population was covered by Medicare, which is designed for seniors. About 9% of the U.S. population has no insurance. Individuals who purchase health insurance on their own account for 7% and 1% of the population is covered under the military.

Comprehensive health insurance policies pay benefits for insureds for preventative care and when they become ill or injured. Managed care is the most common form of coverage. In managed care, insurance companies establish fee agreements with doctors and hospitals who provide health care services.

If health insurance is provided through employment, the employer typically pays the insurer a set amount of money in advance for all health care costs. The employee may have to contribute a portion of the premium to the employer via a payroll deduction. The employee then pays a flat amount for the services as either a copayment or a percentage of the cost of covered services provided.

In most managed care plans, doctors or hospitals are chosen from a network of providers. Some managed care plans allow for visits to doctors outside the network, at a greater cost to the employee.

Some of the largest carriers of health insurance are Blue Cross Blue Shield plans and publicly traded companies. Blue Cross Blue Shield companies operate independently as part of an association. Blue Cross companies originally focused on hospitalization coverage. Blue Shield companies originally focused on coverage for doctor visits. The two associations merged and its independent licensees now provide health insurance coverage options for employer groups and individuals.

Developing Issues for Health Insurers

According to AM Best's annual Review & Preview report on the U.S. health insurance sector, various segments of the health insurance sector face a range of issues:

CHAPTER 4: HEALTH

For commercial products overall, premiums had grown substantially over the past decade while enrollment trends have fluctuated by segment. In 2020, new premium trends flattened somewhat due to COVID. However, most carriers indicated that individuals and groups were sticking with their existing carriers during the crisis, which effectively dampened new sales while simultaneously having a positive impact on persistency, as reported consistently across health insurers. However, the commercial market share as a percentage of overall total medical premium (including Managed Medicaid, Medicare Advantage, and the Federal Employees Health Benefits Program) has declined steadily, from 56% in 2009 to under 40% in 2019. The drop was not unexpected by AM Best, given the growth in government programs driven by Medicaid expansion and the growing senior population aging into Medicare, which has fueled rapid growth in both those core medical market segments. In addition more employer groups have moved to administrative only (ASO) or self-insured contracts in which the health insurer only administered the health plan and the employer is responsible for claim payments.

Individual Segment: Since the rollout of the ACA, the individual commercial market has had its challenges. The segment has seen problems with website navigation, fluctuations in enrollment, and sizable financial losses for insurers. For health insurers, after several years of high double-digit rate increases, as well as successful initiatives to enroll members with chronic conditions in disease-management programs to ensure that they received the proper care, the individual line turned profitable several years ago, with record profitability in 2018. Rates filed in 2019 to be applied in 2020 also featured some of the lowest requested rate increases since inception, and some states even saw requests to cut rates. In March 2021, Congress passed the American Rescue Plan, which increased subsidies for many individuals for ACA individual coverage. The increased subsidies should lower premiums for a large number of individuals and may increase individual enrollment.

Group Segment: The fully insured employer group segment, including both large and small group markets, has been consistently profitable the last few years, with a record year in 2020 for many health insurers. AM Best expects the positive trends to continue, although margins may contract due to factors such as a return to more normalized utilization and the lack of a widespread deferral of elective and non-urgent care that occurred in the first half of 2020; the ongoing shift to self-insured coverage; unknowns such as future COVID waves and the impact on utilization; and the rise in prescription drug prices. Margins for the fully insured group business have been tight, with large group business averaging just over 1% over the last five years, while small group business has trended up toward 4%.

Consolidated membership and revenue growth for group health insurance has been limited for many years. More employers currently elect to self-insure employee health benefits and an increased number of small group employers no longer offer health benefits. In addition, the price of health coverage has become a focal point when employers look to provide coverage for their employees. Many employers have implemented benefit modifications to lower the impact of premium rate increases at renewal, as well as increased employee cost sharing.

Medicaid: After a brief period of Medicaid membership decline through year-end 2019, the pandemic's broad effect on the U.S. economy from business shutdowns and stay-at-home directives early on in the pandemic led to layoffs and furloughs, which had accelerated unemployment rates and started the reversal of this trend. Medicaid enrollment in 2020 and 2021 has experienced significant growth during the COVID public health emergency (PHE). During the period of the PHE, states are not permitted to perform redeterminations, which verify continued eligibility for Medicaid. Once the COVID PHE ends, states will have 12 months to complete the redetermination process.

Senior Market: The increase in the senior population, as well as the popularity of managed care products, which are attractive due to low member-paid premiums and more comprehensive benefits, has driven growth in senior segment premium revenue and earnings for health insurers, a trend which is expected to continue in future years.

Medicare Advantage: Medicare Advantage (MA) premiums grew favorably during the past few years (excluding blue book filers), with an annual growth of more than 10% over the last three years, a trend that is most likely to continue given the aging population in the United States and the increased percentage of Medicare eligible individuals enrolling in MA products versus traditional Medicare. Enrollment has more than doubled over the last 10 years, from 11 million in 2010 to 24 in 2020, showing the growth in popularity of this plan, which captures 36% of the Medicare beneficiaries.

Medicare Supplement: Medicare supplement premium and enrollment grew steadily from 2011 through 2020, reaching over 14 million members and $33 billion premiums. Over one-third of individuals in traditional Medicare have Medicare supplemental coverage. Geographically, more people in rural areas are selecting traditional Medicare with a supplemental plan due to the decreased availability of MA plans.

Major Types of Health Plans

HMO (Health Maintenance Organization): Members select a primary care physician, who oversees all aspects of the members' medical care and provides referrals to see specialists. Most services received from doctors or hospitals out of the plan's network are not covered.

PPO (Preferred Provider Organization): A network of doctors, hospitals and other health care providers make up the organization, but the PPO also allows a member to go to specialists, out-of-network doctors or hospitals without needing prior authorization from a primary care physician. However, more of the costs to receive care outside the network are shouldered by the member.

POS (Point of Service): The member designates a primary care physician but retains the option to receive services from doctors without a referral or go outside the network for care and shoulder a larger portion of the cost.

Fee-for-service health plans, or indemnity plans, were once the traditional route for coverage. There is no network of pre-approved providers, so a member can choose to visit any doctor or hospital. These plans cost the most and have dwindled sharply in the past 30 years.

Some insurers offer plans that combine a high-deductible health plan (HDHP) with a pretax health savings account (HSA). The HSA pays for qualified and routine health care expenses with tax-free money until the deductible is met; then the insurance coverage takes over. The funds in the HSA also can be used for expenses the HDHP doesn't cover, and HSA balances carry forward to future years.

Products and Terms

Health products come in a wide variety of forms and address basic health needs, ranging from preventative and basic medical care to specialized forms of illness and accident coverage. Health products include:

Indemnity Health Plans: These may be offered on an individual or group basis. Indemnity plans allow members to choose their own doctor or hospital. The carrier then pays a fixed portion of total charges. Indemnity plans are often known as "fee-for-service" plans.

High-Deductible Health Plans: These may feature low premiums and an integrated deductible for both medical and pharmacy costs. Some plans combine a health plan with a Health Savings Account.

Health Savings Accounts: Participants and/or their employers may contribute pretax money to be used for qualified medical expenses. HSAs, which are portable, must be linked to a high-deductible health insurance policy.

Health Reimbursement Arrangements: HRAs are funds provided by the employer that employees utilize for covered services. Any leftover funds can carry over from year to year. However, HRAs are not portable.

Dental Plans: Traditional dental plans may help cover preventive, basic and major services.

CHAPTER 4: HEALTH

Dental Preferred Provider Organizations: These offer discounts to members who use in-network dental providers.

Vision Plans: Vision care plans may cover regular eye exams, treatment for conditions and assistance with corrective lenses.

Pharmacy: Plans may cover part or all of prescription drug costs.

Flexible Spending Account: A program where employees may contribute pretax money to be used for medical expenses, including copays, coinsurance, and any non-covered services or over-the-counter medication. Funds in a flexible spending account cannot be carried over from year to year.

Medicare Advantage: This provides Medicare-eligible individuals the benefits of traditional Medicare, plus additional features and benefits such as wellness program and case management services. Individuals who select Medicare Advantage agree to use in-network doctors and hospitals or face much higher out-of pocket costs.

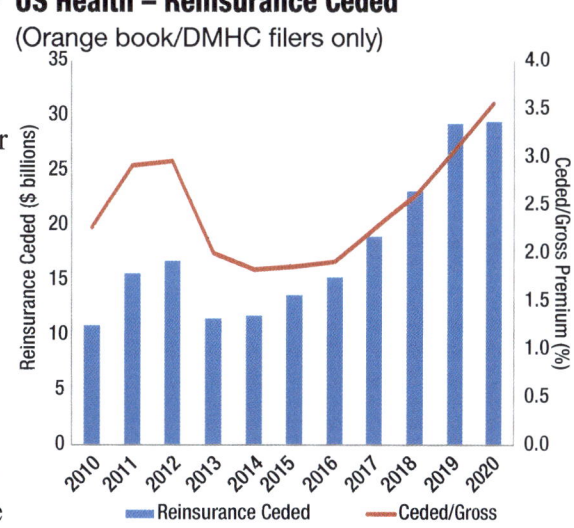

US Health – Reinsurance Ceded
(Orange book/DMHC filers only)

Source: AM Best data and research

Common Health Insurance Terms

Coinsurance: For health insurance, it is a percentage of each claim after the deductible is paid by the policyholder. For a 20% health insurance coinsurance clause, the policyholder pays for the deductible plus 20% of covered benefits. After paying 80% of losses up to an out-of-pocket maximum, the insurer starts paying 100% of losses.

Copayment: A predetermined, flat fee an individual pays for covered health care services, in addition to what insurance covers. For example, some HMOs require a $20 copayment for each office visit, regardless of the type or level of services provided during the visit. Copayments are not usually specified by percentages.

Disease Management: A system of coordinated health care services and communications with members who have certain medical conditions.

SPOTLIGHT

A Healthy Dose of Reality

Exercise has always been a passion for Discovery Ltd. Founder and Chief Executive Officer Adrian Gore. He once took an already grueling travel schedule and added stair running in hotels and airports and between meetings in his office.

In 1992, Gore—just 28 years old—created a unique rewards-based health insurance model to improve individuals' wellness and enhance their lives

Today Discovery impacts more than 46 million lives in 24 markets. The insurtech made a global name for itself with its Vitality business model, which rewards members with inexpensive flights, discounts and other perks for meeting health goals and making positive lifestyle changes such as increasing physical activity, eating more healthfully and getting annual preventive screenings.

Q. How did the idea for Discovery come about, and how is the insurtech using innovation and behavioral science to create a shared value insurance model that rewards individuals for healthy behaviors while driving down health care costs?

A. When we started Discovery in the early 1990s, there was a clear need for a sustainable approach that integrated traditional medical aids and health insurance. That was the embryo for our vision of building an actuarially sound health insurance organization focused on demand-side management—namely, making people healthier.

At the time, behavioral economics wasn't a well-known field, but we had an intellectual hunch that we could incentivize people to adopt healthier behaviors and embed that into our business model. Over time, the data and results confirmed that hunch. We came to understand that people's behavioral biases around wellness, such as putting off that run or healthy food choice, acted against their own best interests, and we sought to nudge people in the right direction through a behavior change model called Vitality.

The Vitality model is unique in that it prices the value created through behavior change into the cost of insurance. It provides clients with personalized goals, rewards them for meeting goals, captures the economic value created or lower claims, and shares that value with clients by using it to fund the incentives and rewards that drive healthier behavior.

Adrian Gore

The Vitality model has been proven to drive better health care outcomes, with highly engaged members demonstrating 10% lower hospital admissions, 10% to 30% lower hospital costs and 25% shorter hospital stays. Vitality members in South Africa live 14 years longer than the average insured population. Reinsurers have also validated the long-term mortality impact of Vitality, with members having, on average, 42% improved mortality rates, and highly engaged members showing a 76% reduction in mortality.

Similarly, in our auto insurance offering, highly engaged Vitality drivers in South Africa have 63% fewer accidents than the worst or unengaged drivers, and 77% have fewer severe accidents.

The global pandemic has further demonstrated the important role the insurance sector can play in helping keep its customers healthy.

Q. How important is it to incentivize healthy behaviors?

A. Never has our shared value model been more relevant than during the current global pandemic, which has exposed the link between noncommunicable diseases and infectious diseases.

The pandemic has magnified the importance of addressing lifestyle-related risk. Global research demonstrates that more than 50% of COVID-19-related deaths are attributed to individuals with three or more comorbidities, such as diabetes or heart disease. We are now seeing that behavior can determine not only noncommunicable disease risk but communicable disease risk as well.

For example, according to our data analysis of South African cases, a 65-year-old male who does not exercise and has no other chronic conditions has a 55% higher chance of dying from a COVID infection than a 45-year-old with no chronic conditions. In contrast, a 65-year-old male with no chronic conditions and who exercises for 30 minutes four times per week has a risk 22% lower than a 45-year-old who does not exercise at all.

Business models that help make people healthier, while simultaneously lowering the price of insurance, have the potential to make a profound contribution to society by building resilience against both noncommunicable and communicable diseases and helping individuals and health care systems weather severe shocks.

Q. How are you leading your company in this time of disruption?

The rising societal expectations for companies to act responsibly have now reached a climax. There is now a fundamental recognition that the purpose of business cannot be narrowly focused on making money without regard for how it interacts with the sustainability and well-being of the societies and environments in which it operates.

—Lori Chordas

CHAPTER 5: REINSURANCE/ART

Overview of Reinsurance

Broadly put, reinsurance is insurance for insurers.

Insurance companies face many risks in their daily operations, including:

- **Asset risks**, or the changing nature of investment values.
- **Credit risk,** or the obligations owed by customers and/or debtors.
- **Liability risk**, or potential losses due to inadequate pricing or reserving, or from catastrophes and other events.

Reinsurance is a transaction that indemnifies the primary insurer against those potential losses. The primary insurer, or ceding company, transfers a portion of risk to the reinsurer. How much risk and what conditions trigger the reinsurance are specified in the treaties. Generally, the primary carrier retains a fair amount of the risk.

Global Reinsurance – Total Dedicated Reinsurance Capital

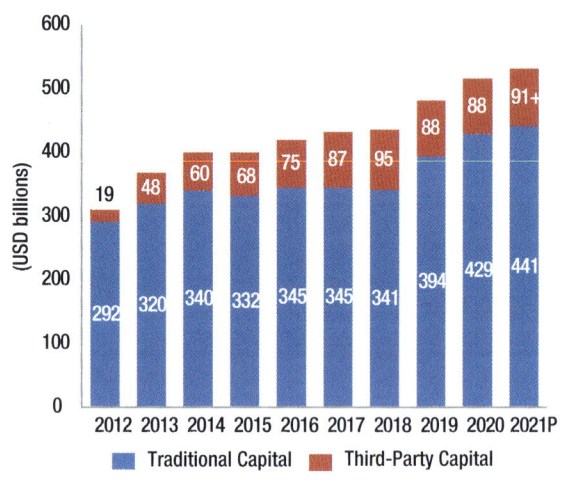

Year	Traditional Capital	Third-Party Capital
2012	292	19
2013	320	48
2014	340	60
2015	332	68
2016	345	75
2017	345	87
2018	341	95
2019	394	88
2020	429	88
2021P	441	91+

(USD billions)

Source: AM Best data and research; Guy Carpenter

Reinsurance allows insurers to increase the maximum amount they can insure. However, most reinsurance contracts do not absolve the ceding insurer's responsibility to pay the insurance claims should the reinsurer fail. The first reinsurance companies were born out of a major fire in 1842 that burned a large section of Hamburg, Germany, and killed at least 50 people. The conflagration exposed the inability of insurers to cope with such a catastrophe, and the insurers recognized the need to distribute risk portfolios among several carriers.

For a basic reinsurance scenario, take an office building worth $20 million. A primary carrier may accept the risk of loss and then turn to a reinsurer, agreeing to cover the first $10 million and ceding the rest. If losses at the building then were to exceed the primary layer of $10 million, say $14 million, the reinsurer would be called upon to cover the remaining $4 million.

In a case like this, the arrangement is said to be a nonproportional agreement, also known as an excess of loss agreement. In proportional agreements, the primary insurer and reinsurer share the liability risk proportionately. In the case of a quota share agreement, the primary insurer and reinsurer split the premiums and losses on a fixed percentage basis.

The two basic types of reinsurance arrangements are treaty and facultative. Treaty reinsurance contractually binds the insurer and reinsurer together, with respect to certain

CHAPTER 5: REINSURANCE/ART

specified business. The treaty requires the insurer to cede all the risks specified by the agreement with the reinsurer, and the reinsurer must assume those specified risks. This means that the reinsurer automatically takes the risk for all policies that are covered by the treaty, and not just one particular policy.

Facultative reinsurance, on the other hand, is done more on a case-by-case basis. The reinsurance is issued after an individual analysis of the situation and by deciding coverage case by case. The reinsurer can determine if it wants some or all of the risk associated with that particular policy. This arrangement usually takes place when the risks are so unusual or so large that they aren't covered in the insurance company's standard reinsurance treaties.

Reinsurers also can purchase reinsurance to cover their own risk exposure or to increase their capacity. This process is called a retrocession.

Developing Issues in Reinsurance

AM Best's annual report on the global reinsurance industry highlights reinsurers' front-row position on product and business innovation.

The reinsurance segment is one of the most innovative due to the level of sophistication in product development and capital management. Reinsurers have become more active at working with insurtechs, several of them effectively digital managing general agent (MGA) start-ups. Volumes involved are still relatively small but growing rapidly. The combination of a low-cost distribution channel and an efficient administration and claims platform, added to robust capital support and underwriting expertise from reinsurers, seems appealing. Start-up expenses and prudent management of technically profitable growth can be a challenge, but this is mitigated by the potential advantages of having access to granular insureds' data in real time, a more refined understanding of customers' behaviors, and abundant opportunities for new product development in a more digitized world.

These initiatives always have the potential of conflict with cedants and brokers.

Global Reinsurance – Estimated Total Third-Party Capital

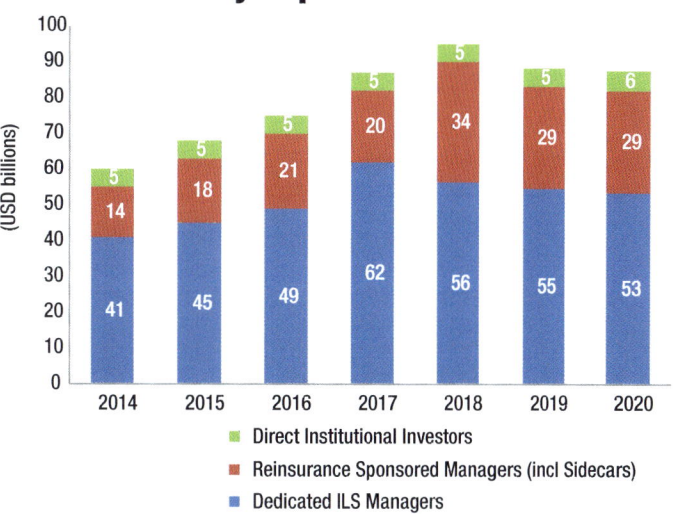

(USD billions)

Year	Dedicated ILS Managers	Reinsurance Sponsored Managers (incl Sidecars)	Direct Institutional Investors
2014	41	14	5
2015	45	18	5
2016	49	21	5
2017	62	20	5
2018	56	34	5
2019	55	29	5
2020	53	29	6

Source: AM Best data and research; Guy Carpenter

www.ambest.com

A common strategy is to operate through very well-defined business units, separate subsidiaries, as a minority investor, or through agreements with third parties. The focus tends to be on new niches, product lines, or customer segments where the likelihood for conflict with previous business partners is minimized. Sometimes brokers and insurers are offered the opportunity to play a clear role as partners, not as competitors. It is a fine balancing exercise. Reinsurers are still investing modestly in these areas, but in a methodical and organized way, with well-defined budgets and close monitoring of outcomes, trying to keep abreast of the latest technological developments to retain relevance.

As for a shift toward more stable results, the most visible changes relate to property natural catastrophe. At reinsurers' request, retention levels have increased, limits lowered, and contract language tightened. Reinsurers' cover has moved upwards in the tower. Closer cooperation with third-party capital for retro cover is evident, thanks to the large size and long-term horizon of the most dominant, committed investors; a lack of other investment opportunities; expected higher returns; and the regulatory efficiency of the capital markets (in particular, catastrophe bonds). Despite third-party capacity having stabilized in the past two years, we see potential for renewed expansion. There is clear interest in diversifying away from nat cat risks toward casualty lines. However, challenges in price modeling remain, as does the mismatch of term horizons between liabilities and investors' expectations. Potential conflict with traditional capital also cautiously interested in expanding into those lines may be another obstacle to significant change in the risk profile of the insurance-linked securities markets.

Alternative Risk Transfer and Risk Financing

The blurring of boundaries between insurance and capital markets is most evident in structured finance, part of an area that is broadly known as alternative risk transfer.

The highest-profile members of the ART community are captives—insurance or reinsurance companies owned by their insured clients and located in jurisdictions, or domiciles, that may be tax-friendly or may have reduced capital and reserve requirements. Captives typically are formed by one or more noninsurance companies when traditional market coverage is more limited, or when the parent companies wish to have more direct control of their own risks.

Structured finance is a complex process of transferring risk, often with the purpose of raising capital. Much of the activity revolves around risk securitization, whereby the involved assets are not used as collateral as is typically found in a loan scenario. Instead, funds from investors are advanced to the originator based on the history of those assets, indicating a cash flow into the originator's business. The assets are then transferred by the originator to a separate legal entity—a special purpose vehicle—that in turn issues securities to the investors. Interest and principal paid on those securities are financed by the cash flow.

CHAPTER 5: REINSURANCE/ART

Insurance-Linked Securities and Structured Transactions

Capital markets participants, reinsurers, brokers and insurers continue to collaborate in various combinations to create new risk-based offerings, including:

Natural Catastrophe Bonds: An alternative to reinsurance, these securities are used by insurers to protect themselves from natural catastrophes. Typically, they pay higher yields because investors could lose their entire stake in the event of a disaster. If the catastrophe happens, the funds go to the insurer to cover claims.

Best's Rankings

Top 25 World's Largest Reinsurance Groups
Ranked by Unaffiliated Gross Premiums Written in 2019
(US$ Millions)[1]

Ranking	Company Name	Life & Non-Life Gross	Life & Non-Life Net	Non-Life Only Gross	Non-Life Only Net	Total Shareholders' Funds[2]	Loss Ratio[3]	Expense Ratio[3]	Combined Ratio[3]
1	Munich Reinsurance Company	45,846	43,096	30,237	29,011	36,845	74.7	30.9	105.6
2	Swiss Re Ltd.	36,579	34,293	21,512	20,636	27,258	78.7	30.3	109.0
3	Hannover Rück SE[4]	30,421	26,232	20,568	17,449	14,543	72.8	29.1	101.9
4	SCOR S.E.	20,106	17,910	8,795	7,695	7,588	70.2	30.1	100.2
5	Berkshire Hathaway Inc.	19,195	19,195	13,333	13,333	451,336	80.8	25.4	106.2
6	China Reinsurance Group Corporation	16,665	15,453	6,422	6,020	15,772	68.0	33.8	101.8
7	Lloyd's[5,6]	16,511	12,213	16,511	12,213	45,010	73.7	33.9	107.6
8	Canada Life Re	14,552	14,497	N/A	N/A	21,137	N/A	N/A	N/A
9	Reinsurance Group of America Inc.	12,583	11,694	N/A	N/A	14,352	N/A	N/A	N/A
10	Korean Reinsurance Company	7,777	5,432	6,427	4,229	2,261	84.6	14.9	99.6
11	Everest Re Group Ltd.	7,282	6,768	7,282	6,768	9,726	76.3	26.7	103.0
12	PartnerRe Ltd.	6,876	6,301	5,377	4,826	7,327	79.5	26.5	106.0
13	General Insurance Corporation of India[7]	6,481	5,773	6,310	5,608	7,289	91.7	21.4	113.1
14	RenaissanceRe Holdings Ltd.	5,806	4,096	5,806	4,096	7,560	74.0	27.9	101.9
15	AXA XL	5,326	4,201	5,326	4,201	13,238	80.5	30.5	111.0
16	Transatlantic Holdings, Inc	5,237	4,845	5,237	4,845	5,377	72.9	30.7	103.6
17	Arch Capital Group Ltd.[11]	4,201	2,995	4,201	2,995	13,929	76.0	35.8	111.8
18	MS&AD Insurance Group Holdings, Inc.[7,8]	3,922	N/A	3,922	N/A	15,007	N/A	N/A	101.712
19	Assicurazioni Generali SpA	3,831	3,831	1,122	1,122	39,056	80.8	29.4	110.2
20	R+V Versicherung AG[9]	3,785	3,785	3,785	3,785	2,641	83.1	24.5	107.6
21	MAPFRE RE, Compañía de Reaseguros S.A.[10]	3,600	3,003	3,004	2,416	2,175	69.1	29.3	98.4
22	Sompo International Holdings, Ltd.	3,580	3,088	3,580	3,088	7,386	67.2	29.5	96.7
23	The Toa Reinsurance Company, Limited[7,8]	3,104	2,579	2,226	1,801	2,792	72.4	35.0	107.4
24	AXIS Capital Holdings Limited	2,809	1,979	2,809	1,979	5,296	76.4	27.4	103.8
25	Validus Reinsurance, Ltd.	2,409	1,823	2,409	1,823	3,439	77.4	27.8	105.2

1 All non-USD currencies converted to USD using foreign exchange rate at company's fiscal year-end.
2 As reported on balance sheet, unless otherwise noted.
3 Non-Life only.
4 Net premium written data not reported, net premium earned substituted.
5 Lloyd's premiums are reinsurance only. Premiums for certain groups within the rankings also may include Lloyd's Syndicate premiums when applicable.
6 Total shareholders' funds includes Lloyd's members' assets and Lloyd's central reserves.
7 Fiscal year ended March 31, 2021.
8 Net asset value used for total shareholders' funds.
9 Ratios are as reported and calculated on a gross basis.
10 Premium data excludes intergroup reinsurance.
11 Based on Arch Capital Group Ltd. consolidated financial statements and includes Watford Re segment.
N/A = Information not applicable or not available at time of publication.
Source: AM Best data and research

CHAPTER 5: REINSURANCE/ART

Sidecars: Separate, limited-purpose companies, generally formed and funded by investors (usually hedge funds) that work in tandem with insurance companies. The reinsurance sidecar purchases certain insurance policies from an insurer and shares in the profits and risks. It is a way for an insurer to share risk. If the policies have low claim rates while in possession of the sidecar, the investors will make higher returns.

Surplus Notes and Insurance Trust-Preferred CDOs: Surplus notes and trust-preferred CDOs (collateralized debt obligations) provide another funding source for small and midsize insurance companies that find it costly to issue capital on their own. These companies can access the capital markets through the use of the surplus notes/insurance trust-preferred pools. Securities in these pools are issued by a stand-alone SPV and sold to investors. The proceeds of the notes are used to purchase the transaction's collateral, which consists of surplus notes and insurance trust-preferred securities.

Embedded Value (Closed Block) Securitizations: An insurer can close a block of policies to new business and receive immediate cash from investors in exchange for some or all of the future earnings on that block of business. The pledged assets remain with the insurer and are potentially available in the event of an insolvency.

Securitization of Structured Settlements: A structured settlement is an annuity used for settling personal injury, product liability, medical malpractice and wrongful death cases. The defendant (typically, a liability insurer) discharges its obligation by purchasing an annuity from a highly rated life insurance company. Securitization of annuity cash flows is achieved through the use of a bankruptcy-remote SPV. The issuer of the securities, the SPV, raises funds from investors that are used to purchase annuity cash flows from the annuitants. The cash flows received by the issuer are used primarily to service the principal and interest payments due the investors.

Mortality Catastrophe Bonds: Investors in these bonds lose money only if a level of

Global Reinsurance – Combined Ratio

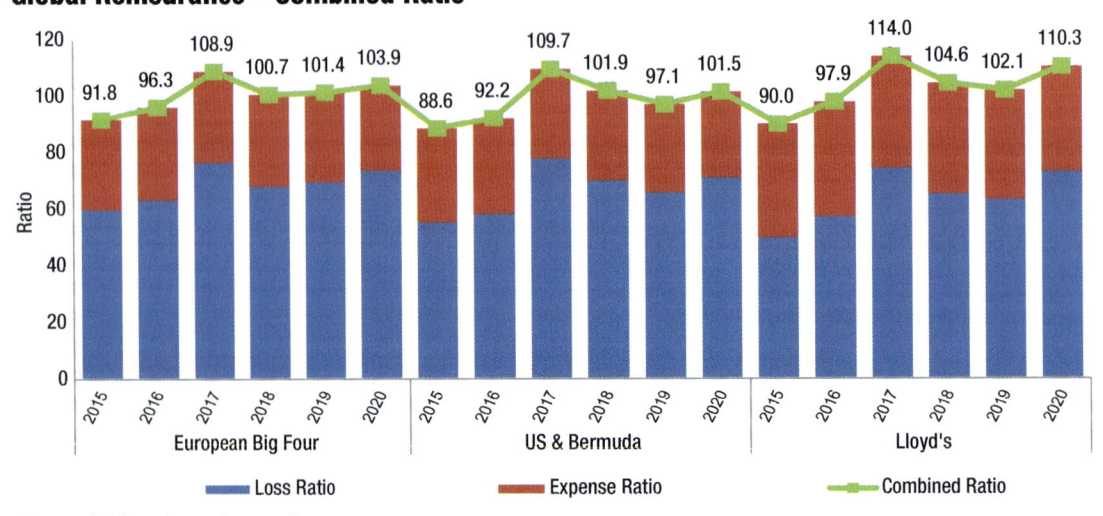

Region	Year	Combined Ratio
European Big Four	2015	91.8
European Big Four	2016	96.3
European Big Four	2017	108.9
European Big Four	2018	100.7
European Big Four	2019	101.4
European Big Four	2020	103.9
US & Bermuda	2015	88.6
US & Bermuda	2016	92.2
US & Bermuda	2017	109.7
US & Bermuda	2018	101.9
US & Bermuda	2019	97.1
US & Bermuda	2020	101.5
Lloyd's	2015	90.0
Lloyd's	2016	97.9
Lloyd's	2017	114.0
Lloyd's	2018	104.6
Lloyd's	2019	102.1
Lloyd's	2020	110.3

Source: AM Best data and research

deaths linked to a catastrophic event exceeds a certain threshold. The event's trigger is extreme (for example, a pandemic). These are a derivative of natural cat bonds.

Life Settlement Securitizations: A life settlement contract is a way for a policyholder to liquidate a life insurance policy. A portfolio of these contracts may be securitized to provide a source of capital. However, certain variables, such as regulatory issues and the uncertainties associated with predicting life expectancies, can create obstacles that may slow their path to the marketplace.

Securitization of Reinsurance Recoverables: Insurance and reinsurance companies have been finding alternative ways to reduce their exposure to uncollectible recoverables and reduce the concentration risk associated with ceded exposures. One approach is the securitization of reinsurance recoverables, which involves a structured debt instrument that transfers risk associated with the risk of uncollectible reinsurance to the capital markets. This risk transfer may also be accomplished through the use of collateralized debt obligation technology.

Winds of Change: Derechos, Snowstorms and Other Catastrophes Are Becoming a Growing Problem for Insurers

Deep freezes in Texas and derechos in the Midwest have gotten insurers talking about and moving toward better modeling, risk selection and pricing.

Hours after a derecho touched down in Iowa in August 2020, First Maxfield Mutual President Randy Druvenga was in a whirlwind of his own. From his office in Denver, Iowa, about 68 miles from Cedar Rapids—where the derecho did considerable damage, Druvenga began contacting reinsurers and agency force and assembled staff, adjusters and contractors on the ground. He and his team were prioritizing claims, utilizing estimating software and satellite images to assess property damages, and finding temporary homes for displaced members and livestock.

First Maxfield only writes in the state, so many clients were affected, with one member's house a total loss after a two-story barn from across the road blew off its foundation and into their home. Cell towers were knocked down by powerful winds and "COVID-19 hanging over our heads," added Druvenga, made it difficult to reach some policyholders and get into homes where others were quarantining.

In February 2021, as a historic deep freeze pummeled the southern U.S., Arrowhead Insurance Risk Managers Executive Vice President and Chief Underwriting Officer Niels Seebeck was on the phone with a Texas customer who was standing in his 40-degree kitchen. "I told him to hang up the phone and turn off his pipes before they froze. He didn't know to do that or to winterize his home because storms like these are rare events in that part of the state."

While derechos, or straight-line thunderstorm wind events, are fairly common in the Midwest, last year's 14-hour event was an anomaly in that it spread across thousands of square miles in multiple states, pounded highly-populated Iowa cities including Des Moines and Cedar Rapids and damaged millions of acres of crops in the nation's Corn Belt, leaving insurers with roughly $7.5 billion of unexpected losses, according to Aon.

The winter weather outbreak disrupted businesses and supply chains and left many homeowners in Texas with burst water pipes, damaged roofs and widespread power outages sparked by a crippled electric grid. The extreme weather, which hit the Lone Star State particularly hard, unveiled infrastructure inefficiencies in areas not often hit by severe winter storms, prompting insurers such as the Alpharetta, Georgia-based Arrowhead to scramble to help unprepared insureds.

These deadly events are examples of a growing type of catastrophe, one that Karen Clark & Co. co-founder and CEO Karen Clark calls "non-tail, large-loss" or "not in the tail of the distribution." Unlike a rare event—think, a one-in-100-year hurricane that could cause losses exceeding $100 billion—large-loss, non-tail events occur more frequently and sometimes in areas not typically associated with those perils.

While non-tail calamities don't cause single-event losses large enough to make it into the tail of the loss distribution, Clark said, "collectively, on an annual aggregated basis, insurers now are paying out about twice as much for those events than the long-run expected annual average for hurricanes."

Last year's derecho is the single costliest thunderstorm cluster event on record, according to Aon's Weather, Climate & Catastrophe Insight 2020 Annual Report. Druvenga, who also sits on the board of Grinnell Mutual in Iowa, noted the storm was five times larger than any other single event in Grinnell's history.

Industry reports say the financial toll exceeded that of nine of last year's record 10 U.S. landfalling hurricanes and tropical storms. The first quarter is typically a more benign period for significant cat losses, according to a Best's Commentary, "Potential Record Catastrophe Losses for Texas Insurers Due to Winter Storm Uri." But some industry experts are now seeing a shift

Karen Clark

and expect costly non-tail catastrophes throughout the year to become the norm.

Modeling Changing Risks

Druvenga said the derecho "literally blew some of the models right out of the water due to its severity, enormity and uniqueness." Iowa State University meteorology professor Bill Gallus said in an interview with a Des Moines TV station that most models failed to provide forecasters with a hint as to the impending line of intense storms.

However, just weeks before this year's winter storm in Texas struck, Karen Clark & Co. released the first version of its winter storm model, which estimated the likelihood of an impending $20 billion winter storm loss event—more than six times the yearly average for that peril, Clark said. She added that this year's storm is characteristic of a non-tail, large-loss catastrophe that "was in our model before the event occurred."

"From what our models show, that type of arctic air outbreak winter storm is now likely a one-in-75 loss event," Clark said. "The main thing for insurers is that they don't want any surprises or to be looking in the rearview mirror and have to make model adjustments after a loss."

Risk levels are changing, "and what was once a one-in-100-year event might now be considered a one-in-75-year or a one-in-50-year event today," noted Steve Bowen, a meteorologist and head of catastrophe insight at Aon. More insurers are now being forced "to think outside the box about events that may not previously have been on the radar or those we assumed would never be plausible in our lifetime," he added.

Insurers are trying to get a better handle on those exposures, and "seeking more usable, modelable risk data to help us do that," Seebeck said. "Having extremely robust information will help determine our position and allow us to analyze it to make our portfolios accurate. Today, that's probably one of the most critical things the industry is focused on, and it's something we take great pride in our ability to do."

Druvenga said Grinnell Mutual plans to recalculate prediction models for catastrophic weather, while First Maxfield Mutual will hire additional staff to handle the rise of non-tail catastrophes. "If we're going to put insurance policies in place, we need to be able to service them at the time of loss. Our industry will continue to plan for future events. It's the right thing to do. The worst thing we can all do is sit back and hope that another event like last year's derecho doesn't happen again," he said.

Clark said her firm accounts for climate change and evolving exposures such as non-tail, large-loss perils in its models, "and doesn't rely on historical data to do that." Some industry experts say not all catastrophe models have kept pace with the changing landscape. They are now calling for updates to those models.

Clark expects the rising threat of costly non-tail calamities to force insurers to reevaluate how they price and manage the risk.

—Lori Chordas

SPOTLIGHT

Laboratory of the Minds

Lloyd's roots date to 1688, when ship merchants met in Edward Lloyd's London coffee shop to share a beverage and the risk of doing business. The market evolved over the next three centuries, birthing the term "underwriters"—as risk bearers signed a slip of paper under the description of risk to indicate how much coverage they were willing to offer.

Fast forward to today, when tech companies are working with Lloyd's Lab—an insurtech accelerator—to facilitate partnerships between cutting-edge technology and the traditional world of insurance.

The program brings together 10 or so hand-picked tech companies to collaborate with Lloyd's, where they are partnered with volunteer mentors.

The Lloyd's Lab taps volunteer insurance experts from Lloyd's syndicates to offer insights, help unlock data and make introductions, and help the insurtechs tailor their solutions so they are in line with the Lloyd's market's objectives and values.

Lloyd's has been hosting two cohorts a year, and at the end of November wrapped up Cohort 5, which matched 13 insurtechs with 60 mentors. This cohort included companies based in the U.K., U.S., Ireland, Germany and South Africa.

With both sides signing nondisclosure statements, Lloyd's syndicates can provide data points for the tech companies to use. They also help educate the startups on the ins and outs of the insurance business, and share what kind of products they'd like to see developed. The insurtechs give the insurers a different perspective and a new way of thinking about managing risks and using data.

Competition to enter the program is fierce.

Ed Gaze, senior manager, Lloyd's Lab, said Lloyd's scouts for insurtechs around the world and encourages them to apply for the program. Typically, 150 to 250 hopefuls apply.

"It's really tough to pick the teams," Gaze said.

A core group from Lloyd's whittles the pack to 40 to 60, then hosts a workshop with 15 or 20 insurance market representatives who vote, reducing

Ed Gaze

the pool to 24. That group is invited to "pitch day," where they give a five-minute presentation on what they do, then field questions for another five minutes.

An audience from the insurance market then votes. Winners are invited to the 10-week program. Once in the lab—and unlike the "Great British Bake-Off" TV show—no one is booted from the group. At the end, participants present their work during "Demo Day," a chance to show off what was accomplished during the program.

Normally, the Lloyd's Lab takes place in Lloyd's Lime Street building in London, but the last cohort was fully virtual due to the COVID-19 pandemic and quarantine, Gaze said. "I'm hoping sometime [in 2021] we'll be able to get back to some face-to-face," Gaze said. "We've really missed building the ecosystem that we had in 2019."

Working remotely via video chat has been successful, he said, and several of the tech companies were focused on COVID-related solutions.

Divided by a Common Language

Insurtechs and insurers can face challenges communicating, even if everyone is speaking English. "Sometimes it's just different language and different culture," said Paul Prendergast, chief executive officer of Blink, a parametric technology company and Lloyd's Lab participant.

Insurtechs often have insurance questions that can be quickly answered by the right people, Gaze said. "They come to insurers to both sell themselves but also to get some information back and help improve their products," he said.

The program "really opened up this conversation and closed the gap between insurtech and traditional carriers," said Cathine Lam, another participant and also the lead data scientist/actuary for Metabiota, an insurtech that tracks epidemics and their economic impact.

"It brings people together—carriers who are seeing new, innovative solutions, and also insurtechs with the right subject matter experts in this think tank—to generate unconventional solutions," Lam said. "Before Lloyd's Lab, we had lots of ideas, but it's talking with the carriers that's really helped us home in and focus on what matters."

—Meg Green

CHAPTER 6: FISCAL FITNESS & AM BEST

Insurance Stands the Traditional Business Cycle on Its Head

Most industries work as follows:

- Build product.
- Incur costs.
- Price product.
- Sell product.
- Generate revenue.

But insurance works largely in reverse:

- Build product.
- Price product.
- Sell product.
- Generate revenue.
- Incur costs.

The significance of this reversed revenue/cost cycle is that the product is priced and sold based on an estimate of future costs to be incurred. These estimates can be wrong for any number of reasons, including catastrophes, claim cost inflation, changes in legal climate, newly identified exposures not known at the time the insurance policy was sold, social changes, investment market fluctuations and other factors.

This means that insurers must be very good at predicting the future and very prudent in administering their business over the long term. It directly results in what are known as underwriting cycles. It's also an important reason why the number of insurance insolvencies sometimes spikes in periods following catastrophes or market disruptions.

The insurance industry is less tangible in that the actual cost of its product isn't precisely known at the time of sale. The true cost is determined at a later point, often much later. Yet risk is taken on along with unpredictable, exogenous factors that ultimately determine profit or loss. While insurers gauge the probability of a large catastrophic event or some latent liability, these scenarios still cause a supply shock. A simplified explanation is that the insurance cycle is driven by supply and demand. If capacity is lacking, the price of risk transfer goes up.

The Risk of Financial Impairment

The business of insurance, because of the inverted cycle in which revenues are received well before claims are incurred and must be paid (or even known), presents special concerns. There are a myriad of issues but the basic concern is assuring, to the extent reasonably possible, that insurance policy premiums and deposits received by an insurer today will be properly managed and available for payment of claims and other policy benefits (perhaps many years) in the future.

As a result, the insurance industry is subject to extensive regulation in the United States and in most other countries. In general, regulatory oversight focuses on three primary elements: market soundness, including rate regulation and promoting adequate insurance availability and healthy levels of competition; market conduct, including review of market participant practices to assure proper conduct and fairness in dealings with customers; and financial soundness, including ongoing surveillance of insurance entities' financial condition and a variety of possible regulatory actions that may be taken if there are indications of financial distress.

In the United States, these financial soundness regulatory actions may consist of required company action plans, various forms and levels of regulatory supervision and licensure actions. In certain instances these actions are insufficient and the next level of action involves conservation, rehabilitation and/or insolvent liquidation. Conservation is undertaken in certain cases for the purpose of obtaining control of the entity and conserving assets while a review of the situation is conducted. Rehabilitation is undertaken when it appears that special actions are required to maintain the entity's solvency, but with these actions, solvency appears possible. Insolvent liquidation is judged necessary when it is clear that the entity's assets will not be sufficient to discharge all of the entity's obligations.

According to earlier studies of impairments by AM Best, impairments varied by line of business, with workers' compensation insurers suffering the most impairments. Fraud has been a frequently identified cause, but most failures can be understood as general business failures associated with poor business strategy/execution and weak management.

State guaranty funds exist to cover unpaid claims of insolvent insurers, but these guaranty funds are generally limited in the coverage they provide to certain types of insurance and with thresholds of the amounts they can pay. There may also be considerable delays associated with payments by guaranty funds.

It therefore continues to be in the strong interest of policyholders to choose their insurance provider carefully and to monitor the provider's financial health throughout the policy period. AM Best has a strong role in this effort by providing interactive ratings evaluations on an ongoing basis.

CHAPTER 6: FISCAL FITNESS & AM BEST

The AM Best interactive rating process is voluntary and subjects companies to independent, objective evaluations of balance sheet strength, operating performance and other critical factors. Not surprisingly, impairments have occurred much more frequently with companies choosing not to subject themselves to this rigorous process.

Overview: Best's Credit Rating Evaluation

The foundation of AM Best's credit rating process is an ongoing dialogue with the rated company's management, which is facilitated by a rating analyst. Each interactively rated entity is assigned to a rating analyst. The rating analyst manages the ongoing interaction with company management and conducts the fundamental credit analysis described in AM Best's rating criteria. The rating analyst monitors the financial and nonfinancial results and significant developments for each rated entity or issue in his/her portfolio. While ratings are generally updated on an annual basis, a rating review can take place any time AM Best becomes aware of a significant development that may have an impact on the rating.

The ongoing monitoring and dialogue with management occurs through scheduled rating meetings, as well as interim discussions on key trends and emerging issues as needed. These meetings afford the rating analyst the opportunity to review factors that may affect the company's rating(s), including its strategic goals, financial objectives, and management practices.

Best's Credit Ratings are initially determined and periodically updated through a defined rating committee process. The rating committee itself consists of analytical staff and is chaired by senior rating officers. The committee approach ensures rating consistency across different business segments and maintains the integrity of the rating process. The rating process consists of the following broad components pictured below:

Broad Components of the Rating Process

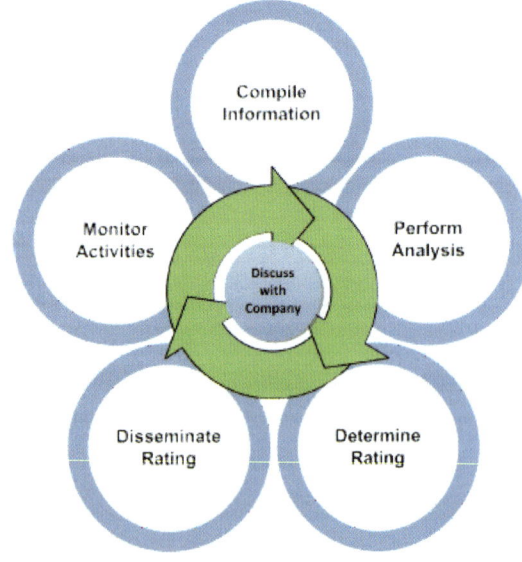

Compile Information

To develop an initial BCR, or to update an existing BCR, the rating analyst may gather detailed public and proprietary financial information and use this information to develop a tailored meeting agenda for a rating meeting. A scheduled rating meeting with the company is a key source of additional quantitative and qualitative information, including the clarification of information previously received or obtained. Key executives are present to discuss their areas of responsibility, including strategy, distribution, underwriting, reserving, investments, claims, enterprise risk management and overall financial results and projections.

Material Sources of Information

In arriving at a rating decision, AM Best relies primarily on information provided by the rated entity, although other sources of information may be used in the analysis. Typical information provided includes a company's annual and quarterly (if available) financial statements, presented in accordance with the customs or regulatory requirements of the country of domicile. Other information and documents that may be reviewed include, but are not limited to: interim management reports on emerging issues, regulatory filings, certified actuarial and loss reserve reports, investment guidelines, internal capital models, Own Risk and Solvency Assessment reports, annual business plans, Best's Supplemental Rating Questionnaire or other supplemental information requested by AM Best, information provided through scheduled rating meetings and other discussions with management, and information available in the public domain. Ultimately, if AM Best is unable to obtain the information deemed necessary to appropriately review and analyze the rated entity (before or after the initial rating release or subsequent rating update) or if the quality of the information is deemed unsatisfactory, AM Best reserves the right to take a rating action based on reasonable assumptions, withdraw any existing interactive rating, or cease the initiation of any new BCR.

Long-Term ICR	FSR
aaa, aa+	A++
aa, aa-	A+
a+, a	A
a-	A-
bbb+, bbb	B++
bbb-	B+
bb+, bb	B
bb-	B-
b+, b	C++
b-	C+
ccc+, ccc	C
ccc-, cc	C-
c	D

ICR = Issuer Credit Rating
FSR = Financial Strength Rating

Note: D is used for non-insurers and securities.
The rating symbols A++, A+, A, A-, B++, B+ are registered certification marks of AM Best Rating Services, Inc.

Perform Analysis

The analytical process incorporates a host of quantitative and qualitative measures that evaluate potential risks to an organization's financial health, which can include underwriting, credit, interest rate, country, and market risks, as well as economic and regulatory factors. The analysis may include comparisons to peers, industry standards, and proprietary benchmarks, as well as the assessment of operating plans, philosophy, management, risk appetite, and the implicit or explicit support of a parent or affiliates.

Determine the Rating

All BCRs are initially determined and subsequently updated by a rating committee. The rating analyst prepares a rating recommendation for rating committee review and deliberation based on an analytical process. Each rating recommendation is reviewed and modified, as appropriate, through a rigorous committee process that involves a rating analyst presenting information and findings to committee members. All rating recommendations are voted on and approved by committee. Rating committee members are all rating analysts who have the relevant skills and knowledge to develop the type of rating opinion being discussed. Rating opinions reflect a thorough analysis of all information known by AM Best and believed to be relevant to the rating process.

For BCRs intended to be made public, the rating committee determination is communicated to the entity (or its representatives) being rated before being publicly disseminated. Private BCRs are disseminated directly to the company following the conclusion of the rating committee.

Disseminate the Rating
The primary distribution method for the public dissemination of BCRs is the AM Best website; in some cases, it may be republished by a press release. Notification of the rating committee determination to the requesting party serves as the dissemination of a private BCR.

Monitor Activities
Once an interactive BCR is disseminated publicly or privately, AM Best monitors and updates the rating by regularly analyzing the company's creditworthiness. Rating analysts monitor current entity-specific developments (e.g., financial statements, public documents, news events) and trending industry conditions to evaluate their potential impact on ratings. Significant developments can result in an interim rating evaluation, as well as modification of the rating or outlook.

AM Best's Insurance Information Products and Services

About AM Best
Founded in 1899, AM Best is the world's largest credit rating agency specializing in the insurance industry. Headquartered in the United States, the company does business in over 100 countries with regional offices in London, Amsterdam, Dubai, Hong Kong, Singapore and Mexico City.

AM Best Rating Services assesses the creditworthiness of and/or reports on over 16,000 insurance companies worldwide. Our commentary, research and analysis provide additional insight.

AM Best Information Services integrates credit ratings, commentary, research and analysis with insurance news, financial data and thought leadership to help consumers and professionals make informed personal and business decisions.

Below are some of AM Best's wide array of products and services. For more information, visit www.ambest.com/sales.

CHAPTER 6: FISCAL FITNESS & AM BEST

Best's Insurance Reports® is an indispensable resource for understanding the creditworthiness and financial strength of insurance companies. It offers the details and analysis behind Best's Credit Ratings, the latest financial data and company information, along with tools and features to enhance your research.

Best's Financial Suite offers quality, detailed data, insurer ratings and analytical tools for top-tier research. Take advantage of our unique perspective to get a complete picture of the insurance industry. Available data includes:

- Global
- US
- Solvency II
- Canada

Best's Capital Adequacy Ratio Model – P/C, US and Global let you evaluate an insurer's capitalization and risk profile with a model that is consistent with the methodology used by AM Best analysts, capturing the combined impact of financial risks associated with adverse market conditions.

GUIDE TO BEST'S FINANCIAL STRENGTH RATINGS – (FSR)

A Best's Financial Strength Rating (FSR) is an independent opinion of an insurer's financial strength and ability to meet its ongoing insurance policy and contract obligations. An FSR is not assigned to specific insurance policies or contracts and does not address any other risk, including, but not limited to, an insurer's claims-payment policies or procedures; the ability of the insurer to dispute or deny claims payment on grounds of misrepresentation or fraud; or any specific liability contractually borne by the policy or contract holder. An FSR is not a recommendation to purchase, hold or terminate any insurance policy, contract or any other financial obligation issued by an insurer, nor does it address the suitability of any particular policy or contract for a specific purpose or purchaser. In addition, an FSR may be displayed with a rating identifier, modifier or affiliation code that denotes a unique aspect of the opinion.

Best's Financial Strength Rating (FSR) Scale

Rating Categories	Rating Symbols	Rating Notches*	Category Definitions
Superior	A+	A++	Assigned to insurance companies that have, in our opinion, a superior ability to meet their ongoing insurance obligations.
Excellent	A	A-	Assigned to insurance companies that have, in our opinion, an excellent ability to meet their ongoing insurance obligations.
Good	B+	B++	Assigned to insurance companies that have, in our opinion, a good ability to meet their ongoing insurance obligations.
Fair	B	B-	Assigned to insurance companies that have, in our opinion, a fair ability to meet their ongoing insurance obligations. Financial strength is vulnerable to adverse changes in underwriting and economic conditions.
Marginal	C+	C++	Assigned to insurance companies that have, in our opinion, a marginal ability to meet their ongoing insurance obligations. Financial strength is vulnerable to adverse changes in underwriting and economic conditions.
Weak	C	C-	Assigned to insurance companies that have, in our opinion, a weak ability to meet their ongoing insurance obligations. Financial strength is very vulnerable to adverse changes in underwriting and economic conditions.
Poor	D	-	Assigned to insurance companies that have, in our opinion, a poor ability to meet their ongoing insurance obligations. Financial strength is extremely vulnerable to adverse changes in underwriting and economic conditions.

* Each Best's Financial Strength Rating Category from "A+" to "C" includes a Rating Notch to reflect a gradation of financial strength within the category. A Rating Notch is expressed with either a second plus "+" or a minus "-".

Financial Strength Non-Rating Designations

Designation Symbols	Designation Definitions
E	Status assigned to insurers that are publicly placed, via court order into conservation or rehabilitation, or the international equivalent, or in the absence of a court order, clear regulatory action has been taken to delay or otherwise limit policyholder payments.
F	Status assigned to insurers that are publicly placed via court order into liquidation after a finding of insolvency, or the international equivalent.
S	Status assigned to rated insurance companies to suspend the outstanding FSR when sudden and significant events impact operations and rating implications cannot be evaluated due to a lack of timely or adequate information; or in cases where continued maintenance of the previously published rating opinion is in violation of evolving regulatory requirements.
NR	Status assigned to insurance companies that are not rated; may include previously rated insurance companies or insurance companies that have never been rated by AM Best.

Rating Disclosure – Use and Limitations

A Best's Credit Rating (BCR) is a forward-looking independent and objective opinion regarding an insurer's, issuer's or financial obligation's relative creditworthiness. The opinion represents a comprehensive analysis consisting of a quantitative and qualitative evaluation of balance sheet strength, operating performance, business profile and enterprise risk management or, where appropriate, the specific nature and details of a security. Because a BCR is a forward-looking opinion as of the date it is released, it cannot be considered as a fact or guarantee of future credit quality and therefore cannot be described as accurate or inaccurate. A BCR is a relative measure of risk that implies credit quality and is assigned using a scale with a defined population of categories and notches. Entities or obligations assigned the same BCR symbol developed using the same scale, should not be viewed as completely identical in terms of credit quality. Alternatively, they are alike in category (or notches within a category), but given there is a prescribed progression of categories (and notches) used in assigning the ratings of a much larger population of entities or obligations, the categories (notches) cannot mirror the precise subtleties of risk that are inherent within similarly rated entities or obligations. While a BCR reflects the opinion of A.M. Best Rating Services, Inc. (AM Best) of relative creditworthiness, it is not an indicator or predictor of defined impairment or default probability with respect to any specific insurer, issuer or financial obligation. A BCR is not investment advice, nor should it be construed as a consulting or advisory service, as such; it is not intended to be utilized as a recommendation to purchase, hold or terminate any insurance policy, contract, security or any other financial obligation, nor does it address the suitability of any particular policy or contract for a specific purpose or purchaser. Users of a BCR should not rely on it in making any investment decision; however, if used, the BCR must be considered as only one factor. Users must make their own evaluation of each investment decision. A BCR opinion is provided on an "as is" basis without any expressed or implied warranty. In addition, a BCR may be changed, suspended or withdrawn at any time for any reason at the sole discretion of AM Best.

For the most current version, visit www.ambest.com/ratings/index.html. BCRs are distributed via the AM Best website at *www.ambest.com*. For additional information regarding the development of a BCR and other rating-related information and definitions, including outlooks, modifiers, identifiers and affiliation codes, please refer to the report titled "Guide to Best's Credit Ratings" available at no charge on the AM Best website. BCRs are proprietary and may not be reproduced without permission.

Copyright © 2021 by A.M. Best Company, Inc. and/or its affiliates. ALL RIGHTS RESERVED.   Version 121719

www.ambest.com

CHAPTER 6: FISCAL FITNESS & AM BEST

GUIDE TO BEST'S ISSUER CREDIT RATINGS – (ICR)

A Best's Issuer Credit Rating (ICR) is an independent opinion of an entity's ability to meet its ongoing financial obligations and can be issued on either a long- or short-term basis. A Long-Term ICR is an opinion of an entity's ability to meet its ongoing senior financial obligations, while a Short-Term ICR is an opinion of an entity's ability to meet its ongoing financial obligations with original maturities generally less than one year. An ICR is an opinion regarding the relative future credit risk of an entity. Credit risk is the risk that an entity may not meet its contractual financial obligations as they come due. An ICR does not address any other risk. In addition, an ICR is not a recommendation to buy, sell or hold any securities, contracts or any other financial obligations, nor does it address the suitability of any particular financial obligation for a specific purpose or purchaser. An ICR may be displayed with a rating identifier or modifier that denotes a unique aspect of the opinion.

Best's Long-Term Issuer Credit Rating (Long-Term ICR) Scale

Rating Categories	Rating Symbols	Rating Notches*	Category Definitions
Exceptional	aaa	-	Assigned to entities that have, in our opinion, an exceptional ability to meet their ongoing senior financial obligations.
Superior	aa	aa+ / aa-	Assigned to entities that have, in our opinion, a superior ability to meet their ongoing senior financial obligations.
Excellent	a	a+ / a-	Assigned to entities that have, in our opinion, an excellent ability to meet their ongoing senior financial obligations.
Good	bbb	bbb+ / bbb-	Assigned to entities that have, in our opinion, a good ability to meet their ongoing senior financial obligations.
Fair	bb	bb+ / bb-	Assigned to entities that have, in our opinion, a fair ability to meet their ongoing senior financial obligations. Credit quality is vulnerable to adverse changes in industry and economic conditions.
Marginal	b	b+ / b-	Assigned to entities that have, in our opinion, a marginal ability to meet their ongoing senior financial obligations. Credit quality is vulnerable to adverse changes in industry and economic conditions.
Weak	ccc	ccc+ / ccc-	Assigned to entities that have, in our opinion, a weak ability to meet their ongoing senior financial obligations. Credit quality is vulnerable to adverse changes in industry and economic conditions.
Very Weak	cc	-	Assigned to entities that have, in our opinion, a very weak ability to meet their ongoing senior financial obligations. Credit quality is very vulnerable to adverse changes in industry and economic conditions.
Poor	c	-	Assigned to entities that have, in our opinion, a poor ability to meet their ongoing senior financial obligations. Credit quality is extremely vulnerable to adverse changes in industry and economic conditions.

* Best's Long-Term Issuer Credit Rating Categories from "aa" to "ccc" include Rating Notches to reflect a gradation within the category to indicate whether credit quality is near the top or bottom of a particular Rating Category. Rating Notches are expressed with a "+" (plus) or "-" (minus).

Best's Short-Term Issuer Credit Rating (Short-Term ICR) Scale

Rating Categories	Rating Symbols	Category Definitions
Strongest	AMB-1+	Assigned to entities that have, in our opinion, the strongest ability to repay their short-term financial obligations.
Outstanding	AMB-1	Assigned to entities that have, in our opinion, an outstanding ability to repay their short-term financial obligations.
Satisfactory	AMB-2	Assigned to entities that have, in our opinion, a satisfactory ability to repay their short-term financial obligations.
Adequate	AMB-3	Assigned to entities that have, in our opinion, an adequate ability to repay their short-term financial obligations; however, adverse industry or economic conditions likely will reduce their capacity to meet their financial commitments.
Questionable	AMB-4	Assigned to entities that have, in our opinion, questionable credit quality and are vulnerable to adverse economic or other external changes, which could have a marked impact on their ability to meet their financial commitments.

Long- and Short-Term Issuer Credit Non-Rating Designations

Designation Symbols	Designation Definitions
d	Status assigned to entities (excluding insurers) that are in default or when a bankruptcy petition or similar action has been filed and made public.
e	Status assigned to insurers that are publicly placed, via court order into conservation or rehabilitation, or the international equivalent, or in the absence of a court order, clear regulatory action has been taken to delay or otherwise limit policyholder payments.
f	Status assigned to insurers that are publicly placed via court order into liquidation after a finding of insolvency, or the international equivalent.
s	Status assigned to rated entities to suspend the outstanding ICR when sudden and significant events impact operations and rating implications cannot be evaluated due to a lack of timely or adequate information; or in cases where continued maintenance of the previously published rating opinion is in violation of evolving regulatory requirements.
nr	Status assigned to entities that are not rated; may include previously rated entities or entities that have never been rated by AM Best.

Rating Disclosure: Use and Limitations

A Best's Credit Rating (BCR) is a forward-looking independent and objective opinion regarding an insurer's, issuer's or financial obligation's relative creditworthiness. The opinion represents a comprehensive analysis consisting of a quantitative and qualitative evaluation of balance sheet strength, operating performance, business profile and enterprise risk management or, where appropriate, the specific nature and details of a security. Because a BCR is a forward-looking opinion as of the date it is released, it cannot be considered as a fact or guarantee of future credit quality and therefore cannot be described as accurate or inaccurate. A BCR is a relative measure of risk that implies credit quality and is assigned using a scale with a defined population of categories and notches. Entities or obligations assigned the same BCR symbol developed using the same scale, should not be viewed as completely identical in terms of credit quality. Alternatively, they are alike in category (or notches within a category), but given there is a prescribed progression of categories (and notches) used in assigning the ratings of a much larger population of entities or obligations, the categories (notches) cannot mirror the precise subtleties of risk that are inherent within similarly rated entities or obligations. While a BCR reflects the opinion of A.M. Best Rating Services, Inc. (AM Best) of relative creditworthiness, it is not an indicator or predictor of defined impairment or default probability with respect to any specific insurer, issuer or financial obligation. A BCR is not investment advice, nor should it be construed as a consulting or advisory service, as such; it is not intended to be utilized as a recommendation to purchase, hold or terminate any insurance policy, contract, security or any other financial obligation, nor does it address the suitability of any particular policy or contract for a specific purpose or purchaser. Users of a BCR should not rely on it in making any investment decision; however, if used, the BCR must be considered as only one factor. Users must make their own evaluation of each investment decision. A BCR opinion is provided on an "as is" basis without any expressed or implied warranty. In addition, a BCR may be changed, suspended or withdrawn at any time for any reason at the sole discretion of AM Best.

For the most current version, visit www.ambest.com/ratings/index.html. BCRs are distributed via the AM Best website at *www.ambest.com*. For additional information regarding the development of a BCR and other rating-related information and definitions, including outlooks, modifiers, identifiers and affiliation codes, please refer to the report titled "Guide to Best's Credit Ratings" available at no charge on the AM Best website. BCRs are proprietary and may not be reproduced without permission.

Copyright © 2021 by A.M. Best Company, Inc. and/or its affiliates. ALL RIGHTS RESERVED.

Version 121719

CHAPTER 6: FISCAL FITNESS & AM BEST

Best's Aggregates & Averages lets you benchmark insurance company performance against industry aggregates, and observe industry trends.

Underwriting & Loss Control Resources presents reports on hundreds of businesses and municipal services, written from the underwriter's and loss control manager's point of view.

Best's News & Research Service provides access to a full spectrum of industry research, analysis, and news published by AM Best on the global insurance market.

Other products and services include:

Ratings
- *Best's Credit Ratings - Feed*
- *Best's Credit Ratings Mobile App*
- *Best's Custom Services*

News & Research
- *Best's Review*
- *Reports, Research and Rankings*
- *Multimedia Resources*

Data Analytics
- *Best's Custom Services*
- *Best's Credit Reports*
- *Best's Financial Reports*
- *Best's Library Center*

Rate Filing Information
- *Best's State Rate Filings®*

Regulatory Filing Application
- *BestESP®*

Additional Services & Programs
- *Advertising Opportunities*
- *Best's Insurance Professional Resources*
- *Best's Preferred Publisher Program*
- *Best's Regulatory Center*
- *Redistribution*
- *Tools to Leverage Your Best's Credit Rating*

To learn more about AM Best products and services, contact our Customer Support Services department via email or at (800) 424-2378 or (908) 439-2200, ext. 5742, 8:30 a.m. to 4:30 p.m. ET.

SPOTLIGHT

The Greening of Insurance Asset Management

The Push for Responsible Investing

From the United Nations to nations and states, regulators and representatives are aligning investing standards with concerns about climate risk and social responsibility. Insurance and asset management experts explore emerging standards and expectations, along with the strategies and products designed to lower the stress of complying.

The insurance industry controls trillions of dollars of assets, mostly invested in low-profile, stable monetary vehicles that fly under the radar. But these investments now are attracting greater scrutiny related to their impact on environmental, social and governance issues.

The so-called ESG movement—which involves regulators, social and environmental activists, and even the broader public—is shaping industries across the world. Asset management, banking, venture capital, energy and manufacturing businesses have joined insurers working to balance financial needs with all three aspects of ESG.

Job No. 1 for insurers is to maintain sufficient financial strength to satisfy obligations to policyholders. In other words, they need enough available capital to pay claims. Insurers traditionally have sought investments that offer sufficient returns and appropriate risks. For centuries, those investments included energy, carbon-based fuels, weapons, tobacco and industries now associated with human rights concerns or other sensitive issues.

Many insurers have begun altering their investment practices to avoid areas that have fallen out of favor in recent years, but a growing body of regulators, legislators, activists and other stakeholders is applying significant pressure to incorporate ESG in all areas of the business.

Inflection Point

Many insurers see their choice of investments as a key element in meeting ESG standards. Political changes are amplifying that focus, said Sean Kevelighan, president and chief executive officer of the Insurance Information Institute.

Most of insurers' revenue comes from investments, which can be a great tool for building communities, Kevelighan said. "You are beginning to see companies

Sean Kevelighan

SPOTLIGHT

proactively look at their portfolios and see whether or not there are ways they can address the issues through their investments," he said. "You're also seeing companies find ways to help their customers with the risks that are increasing too, beyond just our own investments."

The industry has reached an important inflection point where it is going from a detect-and-repair focus to one of predicting and preventing catastrophes, Kevelighan said. Investments play a decisive role in that approach, as does being part of the broader conversation around ESG, he added.

"We're seeing, with the new administration coming into Washington, that climate is part of virtually everything in that administration. Being part of those discussions, making sure people understand how insurance can be a solutions provider, making sure that people understand what risk-based pricing is and why it matters so much. It's a lot for us to do in the climate area, even above and beyond investments," Kevelighan said.

Rising Regulation

Insurers soon will be subject to broader regulatory pressures, according to David Sampson, president and CEO of the American Property Casualty Insurance Association.

"I think there will be a whole raft of new regulations on ESG-related issues coming from the Securities and Exchange Commission, the Fed, and other regulators on public companies," said Sampson. "All of that's going to have an impact on what happens at the state level among regulators, that is likely to sweep in nonpublic companies, mutual companies and other forms of insurance organizations."

The National Association of Insurance Commissioners is sharpening its focus on ESG issues in general, noted NAIC President and Florida Insurance Commissioner David Altmaier. Another regulatory priority for 2021 is the Natural Catastrophe and Climate and Resilience Task Force, which it formed last year.

"The NAIC has always been involved in climate-related risks and natural catastrophes," Altmaier said. "What we did last year was elevate that to what we call our executive level. Bringing some more commissioner-level attention to that issue and exploring ways that we can make our communities more resilient and make our insurance sector more responsive to natural catastrophes and thereby protect the consumers that rely on them."

David Altmaier

SPOTLIGHT

A Global Perspective

A major driver of the increasing emphasis on insurers' investments is Principles for Responsible Investment, the organization that describes itself as a United Nations-affiliated international network of investors working together to implement its six aspirational principles. PRI began operating in 2006.

It was incubated within the U.N. as a grad student project during Kofi Annan's tenure as secretary-general. It later was spun into a standalone nonprofit with headquarters in London. The U.N. supports PRI via two advisory board seats. "Otherwise we're completely independent from the U.N.," said Chris Fowle, director of the Americas for PRI. "There are no budgetary connections or administrative connections.

"For those that follow the science and understand that climate change is real and it's having an impact on our environment and therefore on humans, then I think someone could recognize that these issues will have an impact on investment returns as well," Fowle said. "In many markets around the world, that recognition sort of transcends politics. There are really important sectors that are impacted by climate change, by enhanced recognition of environmental factors, in fact, affecting valuations."

For example, he said: "There will be an important recognition that some companies will be making the transition to a low carbon economy better than others, therefore potentially creating better returns for their investors than others."

"Clearly there are opportunities," Fowle said. "If you think about companies that might have a product or service that enhances a company's ability to successfully make the transition to a low carbon economy, then there should be a financial return and opportunity associated with that."

PRI's goal is to provide evidence, tools and a framework for recognizing these issues and opportunities to change investment processes, and ultimately help investor signatories be more successful for their stakeholders, Fowle said.

— Staff

Chris Fowle

Printed in Great Britain
by Amazon